Contents

MAMMALS

MOOSE

Breeding

Breeding occurs once yearly, between September and October. After a gestational period of about 8 months, females give birth to 1 to 2 young ones who weigh about 11 to 16 grams. Females primarily care for the young. 5 months after birth, the young are weaned after which they remain with their mothers until they are around 12 months old at which time, they become independent.

Appearance

They possess thick, brown fur which varies from having a lighter coloration to a black coloration. Their heads are also long, while their noses are long and flexible as is their upper lip. On their throats, they have a dewlap of skin. Moose have the largest antlers as compared to other animals, which are often shed and re-grown each year. Males are larger than females weighing 360 to 600 kilograms while females weigh 270 to 400 kilograms.

Lifespan

In the wild, 8 to 12 years.

Length

Adult males have a total body length of 2.5 to 3.2 meters.

Adult females have a total body length of 2.4 to 3.1 meters.

Shoulder height, 1.4 to 2.1 meters.

Diet

They feed on barks, roots, twigs, shoots of willows, shoots of aspen, bladderworts, horsetails, pondweed, bur-reed, leaves and stems.

SEA OTTER
Breeding

Breeding occurs all year round with peaks between May and June or between January to March. After a gestational period of 4 to 12 months, 1 to 2 young ones are born. At birth, the young weigh 1.4 to 2.3 kilograms. Females solely care for the young ones without help from the males. When the young attain 2 months, they are capable of diving. At around 6 months, the young are weaned. The young usually remain with their mothers until they are about 8

months old after which they become independent.

Appearance

Sea otters have reddish brown or brown pelage with their guard

hairs having a lighter coloration and their undercoat having a dark appearance. The guard hairs are usually long. Their faces are circular and fury with rounded eyes and ears and short noses. Their whiskers are long and aid them in foraging for food. They have broad paws that are flat and webbed and their hind legs are long. Their forelimbs have retractable claws and are short. They have patches of loose skin underneath their forearms which they use to store things such as food. Adult males weigh 27 to 39 kilograms while females weigh 16 to 27 kilograms.

Lifespan

About 23 years.

Length

Males measure 1.2 to 1.5 meters in length.

Females measure 1 to 1.4 meters in length.

Diet

They feed on crabs, squid, fish, octopus, urchins, mussels, clams, abalone and shellfish.

BROWN BEAR
Breeding

Breeding occurs between May to July. Females give birth to up to 3 young ones after a gestational period of 180 to 266 days. At birth, the young weigh between 340 to 680 grams and are blind, naked and helpless. Parental care is solely the female's responsibility with males not playing a part in caring for the young. When the young are 3 months old, they weigh around 15 kilograms and are 25 kilograms when they are 6 months old. Weaning occurs are around 18 to 30 months after which the young become independent.

Appearance

The fur of brown bear is dark brown but can be cream, yellowish-brown or almost black. Their legs are usually darker coloured. The hairs on their backs are blackish-brown at the base and are whitish cream at the tips. These bears also possess very large claws that are curved with those on the hind limbs being shorter than those of the forelimbs. Adults weigh 80 to 600 kilograms with males being larger than females.

Lifespan

About 20 to 30 years in the wild.

Length

The head to body length of adults is 1.4 to 2.8 meters. Tail length, 65 to 210 millimeters.

Shoulder height, 70 to 150 centimeters.

Diet

They feed on nuts, fruits, bulbs, berries, tubers, fish, carrion, fungus, grasses, sedges, roots, moss, elk, mountain sheep, moose, ground squirrels, marmots and mountain goats.

HUMPBACK WHALE
Breeding

Breeding occurs during winter months in Alaska. Females then give birth to one young one following a gestational period of about 11 months. At birth, the young measure about 12 to 16 feet long and they nurse until they are about 6 months old at which time they are weaned. The young usually remain with their mothers for up to a year before becoming independent.

Appearance

The bodies of humpback whales are black on their upper surface and white below. They possess around 30 broad ventral grooves on their chests and throats. Large knobs are present on their heads, bodies and jaws with each knob having one or two hairs. Humpback whales have long, narrow flippers measuring about one third of their bodies. The flippers are usually scalloped on the forward edge. Their dorsal fin is small in size and is set far on the back of the body. Adults weigh about 36 metric tons.

Lifespan

About 80 to 90 years.

Length

Adult body length, 12 to 16 meters.

Diet

They feed on small fish, plankton and krill.

CARIBOU
Breeding

Breeding occurs in October. Females give birth to up to 2 young ones following a gestational period of around 228 days. At birth, the young weigh 3 to 12 kilograms and they exclusively nurse for up to one month after which they start grazing. Parental care is primarily the female's responsibility. Weaning occurs when they are about one and a half months old. At around early fall, the young become independent.

Appearance

They are medium sized animals with short, stocky bodies and long legs. Their fur usually has a rich brown or grey appearance with a fringe of white hair present from their throat to their chests. The antlers of caribou are usually amber coloured. Males often shed their antlers following mating while females and juveniles remain with their antlers for longer periods. The antlers of females are more straight and do not branch as much. Males usually have larger antlers as compared to those of females. They also develop large white spots around their necks which are mostly seen around the breeding season. Adult males weigh about 150 kilograms while females weigh about 100 kilograms.

Lifespan

About 10 to 15 years.

Length

Adult body length, 150 to 230 centimeters.

Shoulder height, 120 centimeters.

Diet

They feed on leaves, mushrooms, sedges, cotton grass, wood, bark, lichens, fungus and stems.

ARCTIC GROUND SQUIRREL
Breeding

Breeding occurs in late April. After a gestational period of 3 to 6 weeks, females give birth to up six to eight young ones. At birth, the young lack fur and their eyes have a covering. They are weaned at around 28 to 35 days. They usually become independent at around 6 to 7 weeks.

Appearance

They have brown fur which usually has white spots except their on their underside. The underside has an off-white appearance. In spring, their coat has a reddish-brown coloration while in winter, their coat becomes grey-brown, stiff and thick. Their legs are stubby with four toes. Adults weigh 100 to 750 grams.

Lifespan

About 7 to 10 years.

Length

Adult body length, 21 to 25 centimeters.

Diet

They feed on berries, mushrooms, mosses, seeds, lichens, nuts and dry grass.

AMERICAN BLACK BEAR
Breeding

Breeding starts in spring with a peak between June and July. After a gestational period of about 60 to 70 days, one to four young ones are born. At birth, the young are blind and toothless and their bodies are fully covered with fur. Parental care is solely the female's responsibility with males playing no part in caring for the young. Weaning occurs at around 6 to 8 months.

The young usually stay with their mothers for up to 16 months after which they become independent when the mother forces them out of her territory.

Appearance

These bears are usually black in colour but their colour varies to creamy white or bluish grey in Alaska. They possess a pale muzzle that contrasts their fur and at times they can have a white spot on their chests. Their ears are long with less fur and their shoulder humps are also small in size. Adult males are larger than females with males weighing around 47 to 409 kilograms while females weigh around 39 to 236 kilograms.

Lifespan

About 20 years.

Length

Adult males total body length, 1400 to 2000 millimeters.

Adult females total body length, 1200 to 1600 millimeters.

Tail length, 80 to 140 millimeters.

Diet

They feed on fruits, acorns, mast, ants, roots, honey, calves of moose and fawns of deer.

THINHORN SHEEP
Breeding

Breeding occurs between November and December. After a gestational period of around 175 days, one young one is born.

At birth, the young are fully developed and they are capable of re-joining the group alongside their mothers within two days. At around 3 to 5 months after birth, weaning occurs after which the young become independent.

Appearance

Thinhorn sheep have an off-white coloration and their coat has an undercoat of fine wool. They possess guard hairs that are long and stiff. Females usually have small horns that are slender while males have huge horns that are curly. The distinguishing feature between males and females is the horns. Juvenile males resemble females but as they grow older, their horns start growing more rapidly. In winter, the coat of thinhorn sheep is usually thick. Adults weigh about 46 to 82 kilograms.

Lifespan

About 12 to 20 years.

Length

Adult males body length, 1.3 to 1.8 meters. Tail length, 70 to 115 meters.

Adult females body length, 1.32 to 1.62 meters.790 to 90 millimeters.

Shoulder height, 80 to 110 centimeters.

Diet

They feed on grasses, shrubs, sedges, lichens, mosses and willows.

MULE DEER

Breeding

Breeding occurs between November to February. After a gestational period of 6 to 7 months, one to two young ones are born. The young are usually

hidden during the day as their mothers forage and within a few weeks, they begin following their mothers. Weaning occurs at around 5 weeks after birth up to around 16 weeks. The young then remain with their mother for until they are a year old after which they become independent.

Appearance

During winter, they usually have a brownish-grey appearance and they are tannish-brown before winter. Present on their rumps is a white patch while

their tails are small with a white appearance and their tip is black. The coat of juveniles is usually spotted. Males possess forked antlers which are shed around mid-February. Females lack antlers. Adults weigh 43 to 150 kilograms.

Lifespan

About 9 to 22 years.

Length

Adult body length 1 to 2 meters.

Shoulder height, 80 to 106 centimeters.

Diet

They feed on lower tree branches, twigs, grapes, mistletoe, mushrooms, ferns and cacti fruit.

NORTH AMERICAN PORCUPINE
Breeding

Breeding occurs between October to November. After a gestational period of 205 to 217 days, one young one is born. At birth the young weigh between 400 to 530 grams. They are nursed for about 127 days and weaning occurs around this time. Parental care is often the female's responsibility with males providing little to no care to the young. The young attain independence at around 5 months old.

Appearance

They are usually dark brown or black in colour with dorsal hair guards and spines that contain bands of yellow. Spines extend from their heads and to the tail on their dorsal surfaces. These spines are known as quills. Their bodies are stocky with short legs. They also have small faces and short tails. A black line marks the middle of their tail and lower back. Their back quills are black and are fringed with white. Adults weigh 5 to 14 kilograms with males being larger than females.

Lifespan

About 18 years.

Length

Adult body length is 60 to 90 centimeters.

Diet

They feed leaves, twigs, fruits and tree barks.

STELLER SEA LION
Breeding

Breeding occurs in summer months and females give birth to one young one after a gestational period of around 274 days. At birth, the young are about one meter long and weigh around 16 to 23 kilograms. Parental care is mostly provided by the female and males provide protection to the female. Weaning occurs at around 12 to 36 months and at around 3 years, the young become independent.

Appearance

Stellar sea lions range in colour from reddish brown to light blonde with their chest and stomach having a slightly darker coloration. They usually moult their winter fur yearly. The young are usually almost black at birth. Adult males have wider chests, general forebody structure and necks and their foreheads are higher and broader. Their snouts are flat and a

thick coarse mane is present around their necks. Adults' males weigh around 1120 kilograms while females weigh about 350 kilograms.

Lifespan

About 20 to 30 years in the wild.

Length

Adult head to body length, males, 3 to 3.4 meters.

Adult females head to body length, 2.3 to 2.9 meters.

Body height, 62 to 95 centimeters.

Diet

They feed on pacific cod, pacific salmon, octopus, squid, gastropods, fish and atka mackerel.

AMERICAN RED SQUIRREL

Breeding

Breeding occurs between March to May and August to September. After a gestational period of 33 to 35 days, females give birth to one to eight young ones. The young nurse for about 70 days and are weaned when they are 7 to 8 weeks old. Once weaning has occurred the mother casts  the young out to seek their own territory and they become independent thereafter.

Appearance

The American red squirrel has a reddish or brownish appearance on its upper parts which varies depending on the season. During summer, a black stripe is usually present along its side separating the white or creamy fur from the dark upper fur. Their tails are not as thick and are edged with white. Their eyes are large and black and they are encircled by white bands. Adults weigh 197 to 282 grams.

Lifespan

About 5 to 10 years.

Length

Adult head to body length, 19 to 23 centimeters.

Diet

They feed on acorns, seeds, hazelnuts, mushrooms, birds' eggs, fruit, berries, spruce buds and needles, catkins, willow leaves, poplar buds, bearberry flowers and young ones of snowshoe hares.

HARBOR SEAL
Breeding

Breeding occurs once yearly between late winter to late summer and after a gestational period of around 10 months, one young one is born. At birth, the young weigh 8 to 12 kilograms and are covered in fur and mothers bond with the young within the first few hours after birth to establish recognition. Females primarily care for the young with males providing little care. The young nurse for 4 weeks and weaning commences on the fourth week up to the sixth week. Once weaning is complete, the young become independent.

Appearance

Harbour seals with a yellowish coat that has small pale ringed black spots are said to be in the light phase whereas those with a black coat that has dark spots with light rings are said to be in the dark phase. Their heads are large and round and they lack external ears. Harbor seals possess long flat flippers that consist of five webbed digits. Male adults are larger than females weighing 80 to 170 kilograms as compared to females who weigh 60 to 145 kilograms.

Lifespan

About 40 years in the wild.

Length

Adult males, head to body length, 160 to 190 centimeters.

Adult females, head to body length, 160 to 170 centimeters.

Diet

They feed on codfish, hake, mackerel, herring, squid, octopus, crustaceans, crabs and shrimps.

ORCA
Breeding

Breeding is non-seasonal occurring all year round, mostly in summer. After a gestational period of 12 to 18 months, one young one is born. The young are usually nursed for up to 12 months and during this time, they are taught how to hunt. Parental care is primarily the female's responsibility with males playing no part in caring for the young. At around 12 to 24 months, weaning occurs after which the young attain independence. They usually remain in their natal pods after independence.

Appearance

Orcas have black dorsal surfaces and a white coloration extends just beyond the anus on their ventral surface. Present above their eyes is a white spot and a grey spot is located behind their dorsal fin on the back. Juveniles usually have a grey appearance and the white spot in juveniles has a yellow tint. The erect dorsal fin in females and juveniles is about 0.9 meters high while in males, it is 1.8 meters high. Their bodies are streamlined. Adult males are larger than females weighing 7200 kilograms while females have a smaller weight.

Lifespan

Males, up to 60 years.

Females, up to 90 years.

Length

Adult females, 7 to 8.5 meters.

Adult males, 8 to 9.75 meters.

Diet

They feed on sharks, fish, squid, octopi, sea birds, sea turtles, sea otters, river otters, seals and sea lions.

SNOWSHOE HARE

Breeding

Breeding occurs from mid-March to August. After a gestational period of 36 to 40 days, females give birth to 1 to 7 young ones. At birth, the young are fully developed with their bodies being fully covered with fur. During the day, the young usually hide in separate locations. Parental care is primarily provided by the mother with no help from the males. The young are weaned when they are 14 to 28 days old after which they become independent.

Appearance

During summer, the coat of snowshoe hares has a greyish brown or a grizzled rusty appearance with a mid-dorsal line that is black in colour. Their flanks are buffy while their bellies are white. They have a cinnamon brown coloration on their faces and legs. The ears of snowshoe hares are brownish and have black tips and creamy or white borders. Their fur is usually entirely white in winter and their eyelids are black with blackened ear tips. They have densely furred feet soles and their hind feet possess stiff hairs. Adults weigh 1.43 to 1.55

kilograms.

Lifespan

In the wild, 5 years.

Length

Adult body length, 413 to 518 millimeters.

Diet

They feed on green grasses.

MOUNTAIN GOAT
Breeding

Breeding occurs from late October to November. After a gestational period of 150 to 180 days, females give birth to 1 to 3 young ones. The young are usually born in stiff cliffs to protect them from predators. Shortly after birth, the young are capable of walking and weaning occurs when they are 90 to 120 days.

Parental care is solely provided by the female. The young remain with their mothers until they are 9 months old at which time they attain independence.

Appearance

Mountain goats possess a thick coat of white hairs that are intermixed with brown dorsally. Their horns are pure black and thin and both males and females bear horns. In males, the horns curves back to a greater extent than in females. The hooves of these goats are quite large and oval. Black scent glands are present on their horns. Adult males are larger than females weighing 61.4 to 81.8 kilograms while females weigh 56.8 to 70.5 kilograms.

Lifespan

In the wild, 12 to 15 years.

Length

Adult head to body length, males, 155 to 180 centimeters.

Adult females, head to body length, 140 to 170 centimeters.

Tail length, 10 to 20 centimeters.

Shoulder height, 90 to 110 centimeters.

Diet

They feed on leaves, barks, stems, wood, lichens, mosses, woody plants and herbaceous plants.

HOARY MARMOT

Breeding

Breeding occurs once every two years in early spring. After a gestational period of four weeks, 2 to 5 young ones are born. At birth, the young are naked and blind with short hair on their chin, head and muzzle. Females primarily care for the young and males also take part in caring for the young. Weaning occurs when the young are 2 weeks old. The young attain independence at 2 years.

Appearance

Hoary marmots possess black and white fur and the tips of their fur are hoary. A white patch is present between their eyes and rostrum and their nose tip is also white. Their feet are black and a large black cap is present on their heads. They usually molt once per year .Their ears are small, rounded and furred and their eyes are small in size. Their fore feet have well-developed claws. Adults weigh 8 to 10 kilograms.

Lifespan

About 12 years.

Length

Adult total head to body length, 62 to 82 centimeters.

Tail length, 17 to 25 centimeters.

Diet

They feed on sedges, fleabanes, mosses, lichens, willows, flowers and leaves.

MUSKOX

Breeding

Breeding occurs from late August to September. Females give birth to 1 to 2 young ones after a gestational period of 7 to 8 months. At birth, the young weigh 9 to 11 kilograms and are fully furred. Parental care is provided primarily by the female with males playing a part in protecting the young. At around 8 to 24 months, the young are weaned after which they become independent.

Appearance

The bodies of muskoxen are barrel in shape and their legs are short. Their bodies are entirely covered with fur except for the lips and nostrils. The horns of both sexes are cream-colored with black tips they have short tails that are hidden under their fur. They possess guard hairs that are dark and grow

continuously. In winter, they usually have qiviut which acts as their winter coat and is shed in spring. Their legs are white in colour and older muskoxen can have a huge mane of fur on their shoulders. Adult males are larger than females weighing around 300 to 400 kilograms while females weigh 180 to 275 kilograms.

Lifespan

About 14 years in the wild.

Length

Adult males head and body length, 200 to 250 centimeters.

Adult females, head and body length, 135 to 200 centimeters.

Shoulder height, 120 centimeters.

Diet

They feed on grasses, sedges, leafy plants, shrubs, mosses, wood, barks, stems, grains, nuts, seeds, lichens, fruit, flowers and fungus.

AMERICAN BEAVER
Breeding

Breeding occurs in January or February. After a gestational period of around 128 days, females give birth to 1 to 4 young ones. Prior to giving birth, females usually prepare a soft bed within a lodge and uses her flat tail as a birthing mat when giving birth. At birth, the young weigh 250 to 600 grams and range in colour from brown to red to black. Both males and females take part in caring for the young, feeding and protecting them. Weaning occurs 2 weeks after birth. At around

2 years, the young become independent.

Appearance

American beavers usually have a glossy reddish brown or blackish brown coat with fine under hairs and outer protective guard hairs. Their ears are dark brown, short and round. The hind legs of American beavers are usually longer than their forelegs. Both sexes possess castor and anal glands at the base of their tails. Their tails are broad, flat and covered with large scales that are black. Their upper incisors are bright orange in colour and grow

throughout their lives. Adults weigh 13 to 32 kilograms.

Lifespan

About 10 to 20 years in the wild.

Length

Head to body length, 74 to 90 centimeters.

Tail length, 20 to 35 centimeters.

Shoulder height, 36 to 43 centimeters.

Diet

They feed on leaves, bark, stems, willow, maple, beech, poplar, alder, aspen trees, roots, tubers and wood.

RED FOX
Breeding

Breeding occurs in between February and April. Females give birth to 1 to 9 young ones after a gestational period of 51 to 53 days. At birth, the young weigh around 50 to 150 grams and are blind. Their eyes open when they are 9 to 14 days old. Males, females and older offspring play a part in caring for the young. The young leave the den when they are around 5 weeks old and are nursed for 56 to 70 days after which they are weaned. They then remain with their mothers until the fall of the year they were born with females staying for a longer period.

Appearance

Their fur varies in colour from red to deep reddish brown on its upper parts and ashy, white or slaty on their underside. They can also have a pale yellow coloration. The lower part of their legs is black in colour and their tail usually has a black of white tip. The eyes of adult red foxes are yellow while their noses are dark brown or black. Their jaws are more than half the length of their heads. Adults weigh 3 to 14 kilograms with males being larger than females.

Lifespan

In the wild, about 3 years.

Length

Adult head and body length, 455 to 900 millimeters.

Tail length, 300 to 555 millimeters.

Diet

They feed on rodents, insects, carrion, mice, birds and eastern cottontail rabbits.

GRAY WOLF
Breeding

Breeding occurs between February and April. After a gestational period of 2 months, females give birth to up to 6 young ones. The young are usually born in a den often in a hillside. All members of a pack provide care for the young who nurse for about 6 weeks after which they are weaned when they are 6 to 9 weeks old. A few weeks later, the young are moved to an above the ground location where they sleep and play. The young become independent at 2 years and disperse to find mates.

Appearance

Grey wolves typically have an overall grey coloration with black markings and lighter under parts. They can also be brown, red, black or pure white in colour. Their fur is usually very thick with a coarse outer coat covering their soft undercoat. Their backs are silvery grey-brown and their tails are long and bushy. During winter, their fur becomes darker on the rump, neck and shoulders. Their snout is narrow and less robust in appearance. Their ears are about 2 inches long and short with rounded tips. The legs of these wolves are long and their feet are large. Adults weigh 16 to 60 kilograms.

Lifespan

About 10 to 20 years.

Length

Adult head to body length, 102 to 183 centimeters.

Shoulder height, 66 to 84 centimeters.

Diet

They feed on elk. Moose, caribou, deer, beavers, rabbits, snakes, frogs, lizards, large insects, fish, berries and cherries.

ARCTIC FOX
Breeding

Breeding occurs from April to July. After a gestational period of 46 to 58 days, around 9 young ones are born. They nurse until when they are capable of taking solid foods. Weaning occurs at 28 to 60 days after birth. Parental care is provided by both parents with males hunting for food while females care for the young. At around 3 to 4 weeks, the young emerge from the den. The young become independent after weaning but may remain with their parents.

Appearance

During winter, arctic foxes usually have a heavy white coat which is shed around May to a brown coat that is thinner. Their backs, legs and tails have a dark brown appearance while their underparts are buff in colour. Some may have heavy pale bluish-grey coats during winter that becomes a darker shade of bluish-grey in summer. They also have short legs, ears and bodies. Arctic foxes moult twice each year. Adults weigh 1.4 to 9.4 kilograms.

Lifespan

In the wild, 3 to 4 years.

Length

Adult male head to body length, 55 centimeters.

Adult female head to body length, 52 centimeters.

Tail length, around 30 centimeters.

Diet

They feed on sea birds, fish, seals, birds, mammals, insects, eggs, carrion, lemmings, mice and fruit.

DALL'S PORPOISE
Breeding

Mating occurs from February to March and in summer from July to August. After a gestational period of 347 days, one young one is born. The female primarily cares for the young with no help from the male. At 24 months, weaning occurs although the young continue to nurse until they are about 2 years after which they become independent.

Appearance

There are three colour patterns that dall's porpoise can have. They can have a uniformly black or white coloration. Alternatively, they can have intermixed black and white stripes running along the length of their bodies. They can also have a uniformly black dorsal area with white appearance ventrally. This is the most observed pattern. The white patch usually begins behind the flippers. Their flukes, dorsal fins and flippers are black with white tips. Adults weigh 130 to 220 kilograms and both sexes resemble each other.

Lifespan

In the wild, 16 to 17 years.

Length

Adult body length, 1.8 to 2.0 meters.

Diet

They feed on herring, sardines, crustaceans, pacific hake, jack mackerel, squid and mollusks.

BELUGA
Breeding

Breeding occurs once every three years between February and May. After a gestational period of 12 to 15 months, females give birth to 1 to 2 young ones. At birth, the young ones are completely dependent on their mothers. Weaning occurs when they are 25 to 32 months old. Parental care is solely provided by females and males play no part in caring for the young. The young usually attain independence at 2 years of age.

Appearance

Adults have a distinct bright white coloration and lack a dorsal fin which is replaced by a prominent dorsal ridge. Their heads are bulbous and small and they have a short beak with a cleft upper lip. Their bodies are large with a huge layer of blubber. The flippers of males have slightly curled tips while those of females are flat. Juveniles usually have a pale grey or blur colouring. Adults weigh 400 to 1600 kilograms with males being larger than females.

Lifespan

In the wild, 40 to 60 years.

Length

Adult males, body length, 5.5 meters long.

Adult females, body length, 4.3 meters long.

Diet

They feed on salmons, herrings, octopus, squids, shrimps, crabs, fish and mollusks.

AMERICAN MINK
Breeding

Breeding occurs once yearly in winter. After a gestational period of 40 to 75 days, 1 to 8 young ones are born. At birth, the young weigh 8 to 10 grams with a thin coat of fur and they lack the ability to see. Their eyes open at 3 and a half weeks. Weaning occurs at around 6 weeks. Parental care is primarily the mother's responsibility. At around 6 to 10 months, the young become independent.

Appearance

They are dark brown in colour and their throat, chest and chin have white patches. They are covered with soft and thick fur and their bodies are slender and long with short legs and a pointy face that is flat. The neck of American mink is long while their ears and eyes are small. They also possess a long tail that is thick consisting of up to a third of their total body. Their guard hairs and bright and dark-tawny and are nearly black on the spine. Thy have very wavy under fur on their backs that is greyish tawny and has a bluish tint. Their tails are usually darker than their trunks and can have a pure black coloration on the tip. The toes of American mink are partially webbed. In summer, they usually have short fur that is dull and sparse as compared to their winter fur. Adult males are larger than females weighing

0.9 to 1.6 kilograms while females weigh 0.7 to 1.1 kilograms.

Lifespan

About 10 years.

Length

Adult body length, 460 to 700 millimeters.

Diet

They feed on crayfish, frogs, muskrats, fish, shrews, rabbits and birds.

NORTHERN FUR SEAL
Breeding

Breeding occurs from June to July and after a gestational period of 240 days, females give birth to 1 young one. At birth, the young are fully developed, requiring little care. Females primarily care for the young and males play no part in caring for the young. The young are nursed until they are 4 months old when weaning occurs. At around 3 to 4 months of age, the young become independent.

Appearance

Adult males have brownish-black coloration but can be reddish-brown or dark grey. Females and juveniles are grey in colour when they are at the sea and when they are on land, their fur becomes yellowish-brown due to mud and excrement. At birth, the young are usually black with markings along the sides, muzzle, chin and axillary area that are buff in colour. At 4 months, they undergo moulting to become grey. Adult males are larger than females weighing 180 to 275 kilograms while females weigh 40 to 50 kilograms.

Lifespan

Up to 26 years.

Length

Adult males body length, 213 centimeters.

Adult females body length, 142 centimeters.

Diet

They feed on herring, anchovy, capelin, squid, rockfish, salmon, hake saury, rockfish and mollusks.

MUSKRAT
Breeding

Breeding occurs immediately after spring. After a gestational period of less than one month, 5 to 10 young ones are born. At birth, the young are hairless, blind and helpless. Within the first week, their bodies are covered in thin fur and by the second week, their eyes open. When they are 2 to 3 weeks old, they start leaving the lodge. At 3 weeks, weaning occurs and by 6 weeks, the young become independent.

Appearance

They are covered with short under fur which is usually dense and silky and their guard hairs are long, glossy and coarse. They range in colour from dark brown on their heads and are greyish-brown on their bellies. Their tails are long, slender and flattened and are covered with scaly skin. The forefeet of muskrat are small while the hind feet are much larger and are partially webbed. Adults weigh 0.6 to 2 kilograms.

Lifespan

Length

Adult total body length is 40 to 70 centimeters.

Diet

They feed on bulrush, smartweed, duck potato, horsetail, water lily, willow sprouts, roots, tubers, stems, bulbs and leaves.

NORTHERN-RED BACKED VOLE
Breeding

Breeding occurs from May to September. After a gestational period of 17 to 18 days, females give birth to 1 to 9 young ones. Parental care is solely the female's responsibility and males do not take part in caring for the young. Weaning occurs at around

18 days after which the young become independent.

Appearance

They have a light grey pelage with a rusty to reddish coloration on their dorsal surface. During winter, their colour becomes darker. Their tails are dark grey on the dorsal part and are yellow ventrally with dense hair covering. The terminal hairs of their tails are long and dark. Adults weigh 20 to 40 grams and both sexes resemble each other.

Lifespan

In the wild, 6 months.

Length

Adult body length, 130 to 158 millimeters.

Diet

They feed on leaves, bark, wood, stems, seeds, grains, fruit, nuts, flowers, pollen, eggs, carrion and insects.

CANADA LYNX
Breeding

Breeding occurs in January and February and after a gestational period of 56 to 70 days, 1 to 6 young ones are born. Most births occur in stumps and fallen logs and the young weigh about 200 grams at birth. Females solely care for the young without help from the males. The young nurse for up to 5 months and at around 150 days, they are weaned. They remain with their mothers until they are 10 months old after which they become independent.

Appearance

They vary in colour but most are yellowish-brown. Their upper parts have a grey frosted look while the underside is buff coloured. Most have dark spots with short tails that have black tips and are ringed. They have long and thick fur covering their bodies and this is particularly long on their necks in winter. They have paws that are furry and large and their ears are triangular with tips that have tufts of long black hair. Adults weigh 4.5 to 17 kilograms with males being a bit larger than females.

Lifespan

In the wild, 14 years.

Length

Adult head and body length, 607 to 1067 millimeters. Tail length, 50 to 130 millimeters.

Diet

They feed on birds, fish, snowshoe hares and carrion.

COLLARED PIKA
Breeding

Breeding occurs from May to June. After a gestational period of 3 to 4 weeks, 2 to 6 young ones are born. At birth, the young are hairless and blind and females primarily care for the young. The young often remain in the nest until they around 30 days and are weaned around this time after which they emerge

to the surface. Once they are weaned, they remain in their birth territory for a short period before dispersing and becoming independent.

Appearance

Collared pikas have dull grey fur on the dorsal aspect of their bodies with their shoulders and nape having grey patches which creates an indistinct collar. Their ventral side has white-coloured fur. In summer, adults usually have a brown tinge around their necks and heads while the young that are almost the size of adults are usually fully grey. The forelimbs of collared pika are shorter than their hind legs. The soles of their feet are covered with long fur and their claws are curved. Adults weigh 130 to 200 grams.

Lifespan

About 6 to 7 years.

Length

Adult total body length, 17.8 to 19.8 centimeters.

Diet

They feed on leaves, flowers, birds, birds and dung.

WOLVERINE
Breeding

Breeding occurs between February and April. After a gestational period of 7 to 9 months, 2 to 4 young ones are born. The young are usually born in dens that are mostly situated among rocks. Weaning occurs at around 7 to 8 weeks and at around fall, the young disperse to become independent.

Appearance

Wolverines are bear-like with long, dense, dark brown pelage and have a paler appearance on their heads. Extending from their shoulders to join the rump are two broad yellow stripes. On their throats and chests, there are variable yellowish and white markings. Wolverines possess bushy tails. They have broad heads with short furry ears. Adults weigh 7 to 32 kilograms with males being larger than females.

Lifespan

About 5 to 7 years in the wild.

Length

Adult head to body length, 65 to 109 centimeters. Tail length, 17 to 26 centimeters.

Shoulder height 36 to 45 centimeters.

Diet

They feed on moose, caribou, deer, carrion, porcupines, chipmunks, beavers, marmots, moles, gophers, rabbits, voles, mice, sheep, mule deer, coyote, martens, weasels, birds, birds' eggs, seeds, roots, berries and insect larvae.

EUROPEAN RABBIT

Breeding

Breeding occurs throughout the year with a peak in the first half of the year. After a gestational period of 30 to 37 days, 1 to 14 young ones are born. At birth, they are hairless, blind and helpless and are wholly dependent on their mothers for care with males playing no part in caring for the young. Weaning occurs at around 22 to 31 days and the young become independent at around 4 weeks.

Appearance

They have a greyish coat that is sprinkled with black, brown or grey. Their underside can be white or pale grey in colour and they have a white coloration on the underside of their tail. The ears of European rabbits are small and short. Their guard hairs are banded with brown, grey or black and the nape of their neck has a reddish coloration. In juveniles, there can be a white star shape on the forehead. Adults usually have a brown chest patch. These rabbits moult once yearly. Adults weigh 1.5 to 2.5 kilograms.

Lifespan

In the wild, less than 1 year.

Length

Adults range from 38 to 50 centimeters in length.

Diet

They feed on grasses, leaves, tree bark, buds, roots, fruits, flowers, seeds, grains and nuts.

RINGED SEAL
Breeding

Breeding occurs between April to May. After a gestational period of about 9 months, one young one is born usually in subnivean lairs. Parental care is solely the female's responsibility with males playing no part in caring for the young. Within the first week of life, the mother teaches her young one how to swim. The young nurse for about 5 to 7 weeks. Weaning occurs at around 2 months after which the young become independent.

Appearance

Ringed seals possess a dark grey coat with greyish-white or silver rings on their backs and sides and these rings are usually close together. Their bodies are plumpy and their heads are small and round with a short neck that is thick. Their snout is broad and blunt, facing forward and the eyes are closely-set. They possess relatively small front flippers and their claws are slightly pointed. Ringed seals have light-coloured whiskers that are beaded. Adults weigh 65 to 95 kilograms with males being a bit larger than females.

Lifespan

About 25 to 30 years.

Length

Adult total body length 1.1 to 1.75 meters.

Diet

They feed on fish, shrimps, mysids, amphipods, cephalopods and crustaceans.

WALRUS
Breeding

Breeding occurs once every 2 to 3 years between January and April. Following a gestational period of 331 days, one young one is born. At birth, the young weigh abo60 kilograms and are capable of swimming. Parental care is solely the female's responsibility with males playing no part in raising the young. The young are usually weaned at around 12 to 36 months. When the young attain 2 to 3 years, males and females become independent from their mothers with the males joining the male herd while females stay in the female group but are independent.

Appearance

The skin of walruses is thick ranging in colour from yellowish brown to  light grey. They possess huge tusks and their fur is short except at the appendages. They possess whiskers and relatively small eyes. Walruses have front and hind flippers with the front flippers being relatively shorter. Males are larger than females weighing around 1200 to 1500 kilograms while females weigh 600 to 850 kilograms.

Lifespan

In the wild, 30 to 40 years.

Length

Adult male head to body length, 320 centimeters.

Adult female head to body length, 270 centimeters.

Diet

They feed on gastropods, cephalopods, crustaceans, sea cucumbers, shrimp, octopuses, snails, worms, octopuses, squid and clams.

HARBOUR PORPOISE
Breeding

Mating occurs between June and September. Following a gestational period of 10 to 11 months, one young one is born. The young are usually nursed in secluded coves. Lactation lasts for about 8 t 12 months and the young are weaned when they are 5 months old. The young remain with their mothers after weaning and become independent at around 17 to 21 months.

Appearance

The body of harbour porpoise ranges from dark brown to dark grey on top and the sides are light grey. Their bodies are robust and their midsection is stocky tapering to the tailstock. Their snout is blunt and they possess a small mouth which tilts upwards. Their flippers are oval with rounded tips and are of a small size. Their throats and bellies are white with the throat bearing a grey streak and a dark patch is present on the chin. Harbour porpoises have dark coloured flippers that are slightly rounded and dark stripes extend to their eyes from these flippers. Present centrally on their back is a low triangular dorsal fin. Adult males weigh 50 to 55 kilograms while females weigh about 81 kilograms.

Lifespan

About 20 years.

Length

Adult females total body length, 145 to 189 centimeters.

Adult males total body length, 163 centimeters.

Diet

They feed on herrings, mackerel, squid, octopus, hake, cod, Pollack, whiting and sardines.

AMERICAN MARTEN
Breeding

Breeding occurs between June and August and after a gestational period of 220 to 275 days, 1 to 5 young ones are born. At birth, they are not capable of seeing. They open their eyes at 39 days. Females are primarily responsible for caring for the young but it is unclear whether males also take part in raising the young. At 42 days, weaning occurs after which the young attain independence.

Appearance

The head of American marten is grey while their legs and tails are dark brown or black. Their chests have a cream-colored patch and their backs have a light brown coloration. American martens possess large eyes and their ears resemble those of a cat. The fur of American martens is shiny and long while their claws are curved and sharp. Their tails are bushy and cylindrical and they have triangular heads with pointed snouts. Adult males are larger than females, weighing 470 to 1300 grams while females weigh about 280 to 850 grams.

Lifespan

About 17 years.

Length

Adult males head to body length, 360 to 450 millimeters. Tail length 150 to 230 millimeters.

Adult females, head to body length, 320 to 400 millimeters. Tail length, 135 to 200 millimeters.

Diet

They feed on birds, eggs, seeds, grains, fruits, nuts, insects and carrion.

MASKED SHREW
Breeding

Breeding occurs from May to September. After a gestational period of 19 to 22 days, 6 to 7 young ones are born. At birth, they lack hair and weigh about 0.25 grams. By the 10th day, their bodies are covered in fine hairs. Their eyes open at around 17 to 18 days and by the 20th day, the young are weaned. They usually attain independence by the 30th day.

Appearance

They have a grey-brown coloration with a light grey underside. Their tails are long and have a black coloration on top and are pale underneath with a black tip. Their snout is sharply pointed and their eyes are beady. They possess small ears which are usually hidden in their pelage. Adults weigh 2.5 to 4 grams.

Lifespan

About 1 to 2 years.

Length

Adult body length, 101 millimeters. Tail length, 41 millimeters.

Diet

They feed on ants, beetles, rickets, spiders, worms, salamanders, seeds, grasshoppers, centipedes, snails, slugs, fungi and larch sawflies.

BROWN LEMMING
Breeding

Breeding occurs in winter and summer. After a gestational period of 3 weeks, females give birth to 2 to 12 young ones. Parental care is solely the female's responsibility with males playing no part in raising the young. The young are weaned at around 14 to 16 days after which they become independent.

Appearance

They have brown coloration with a reddish brown appearance on the rump and the back. Their heads and shoulders are grey in colour. Their winter coat is greyer and longer as compared to their summer coat. The ears of brown lemming are small and they also have short legs and a short tail. The soles and toes of their feet are covered in bristles. Adult females weigh about 58 grams and adult males weigh about 68 grams.

Lifespan

In the wild, 2 years.

Length

Adult female, 12.5 centimeters.

Adult male, 13 centimeters.

Diet

They feed on grasses, sedges, mosses, bark, berries, lichens and roots.

TUNDRA VOLE
Breeding

Breeding occurs from April to September. After a gestational period of 20 to 21 days, 4 to 8 young ones are born. At birth, the young weigh about 3 grams and are hairless but by the fifth day, their bodies are covered with fur. They open their eyes 11 to 13 days after birth and are weaned by the 18th day of life. Parental care is solely the female's responsibility. Once weaning is complete, the young become independent.

Appearance

They vary from dark brown, grey to lighter shades of rusty brown and cinnamon on their backs and these show a mixture of black-tipped hairs. They are paler on their sides and much lighter ventrally ranging in colour from ash grey to buff to white. Their tails are pale below and dark above. In more open habitats, they are lighter coloured than in forested habitats. Adults weigh 25 to 80 grams with males being larger than females.

Lifespan

About one year.

Length

Adult body length, 118 to 226 millimeters.

Diet

They feed on leaves, wood, bark, stems, lichens, tubers, mosses, herbs and roots.

CALIFORNIA SEA LION
Breeding

Breeding occurs in early July and following a gestational period of 11 months, females give birth to one young one. Females are primarily involved in caring for the young and they nurse the young for up to 2 days after which they leave the young one on the shore to go and feed at the sea. While at the sea, the female spends up to five days feeding and returns to feed her young one. She continues with this pattern until weaning occurs and by one year, the young become independent.

Appearance

Adult female California sea lions are dark brown but may be tan and males have a lighter coloration. The heads of males appear more robust as compared to that of females. The flippers of California sea lions are black and are coated with short black stubble. Their snouts are long and narrow and visible ear flaps are also present. Juveniles usually have a blackish brown coat that moults to a light brown coat which is replaced at around 4 to 5 months with the adult pelage. Adults weigh about 275 kilograms.

Lifespan

About 15 to 25 years.

Length

Adult body length, 2.4 meters.

Diet

They feed on squid, mackerel, rockfish, sardines and anchovies.

BOWHEAD WHALE

Breeding

Breeding occurs between late winter and early spring. Following a gestational period of 13 to 14 months, one young one is born. At birth, the young are 4 to 5 meters long. It is nursed by its mother and weaned at 9 to 15 months. Once females have given birth, bowhead whales usually segregate into groups so as to migrate and the young and their mothers are often in the front group. Parental care is primarily the female's responsibility.

Appearance

Their bodies are large, robust and dark-coloured with white chins. They possess paired blowholes at the highest points of their heads and their mouths are bow-shaped. They lack dorsal fins. Their heads are extremely large and it  possesses a massive triangular skull which it uses to break ice. Their flippers are paddle-shaped and their bellies are peppered with white spots. Present just before their tails is a grey band. Adults weigh 50 to 60 tonnes.

Lifespan

About 100 to 200 years.

Length

Adult male, body length, 14 to 17 meters.

Adult female, body length, 16 to 18 meters.

Diet

They feed on krill, copepods, euphausiids, zooplankton, mysids and ampipods.

FIN WHALE
Breeding

Breeding occurs between November and January. After a gestational period of 11 to 12 months, females give birth to one young one. At birth, the young are about 6 meters long and weigh 3500 to 3600 kilograms. At birth, they are fully developed. They are suckled by their mothers for 6 to 7 months after which they are weaned. At around eight months, they become independent.

Appearance

The bodies of fin whales are long and lean with brown-grey dorsal surface and deep white undersides. On their lower right jaw, they have a white patch. Their backs have a distinctive ridge since the base of their tails is raised. Wrapping around their midsection laterally is their white underside. Their dorsal fin is curved and is located relatively far back on their bodies. Their heads are flat and two blowholes and one longitudinal ridge extend from the tip of their snout to the beginning of the blowholes. Adults weigh 70000 kilograms.

Lifespan

About 75 years.

Length

Adult body length, 25 meters.

Diet

They feed on fish, squid, crustaceans, phytoplankton, herring, capelin and squid.

COMMON MINKE WHALE
Breeding

Breeding occurs all year round. After a gestational period of 10 months, females give birth to one young one. At birth, the young weigh are 8 to 11 feet long and weigh 450 kilograms. The young nurse until they are 6 months old and then they are weaned after which they gain independence.

Appearance

Common minke whales have a dark grey coloration dorsally and are white ventrally. A light grey rostral saddle that is indistinct may be present. Some may have thin blowhole streaks from their blowholes. A shoulder streak is present on their pectoral fins. Thorax and flank patches join ventrally in the mid-lateral region and the thorax patch is brighter than the flank patch. The most distinct feature of common minke whale is a white transverse band on their outer margins. They possess smooth-sided flukes that have a white or light grey coloration ventrally which are bordered by dark grey. Adults weigh 6 to 10 tonnes.

Lifespan

About 50 years.

Length

Adult body length, 10.2 meters.

Diet

They feed on krill, small fish, cod, herring, sardines and mollusks.

SPOTTED SEAL
Breeding

Breeding occurs from January to May and after a gestational period of 7 to 12 months, one young one is born. Females are primarily involved in caring for the young with males providing little to no care

towards the young. The young are nursed for 2 to 4 weeks and weaning occurs around this time. Once the young are about one

month old, the mother abandons them so that they can fend for themselves.

Appearance

They are medium-sized and lack an external ear. Their bodies are streamlined and a thick layer of blubber is present. Their undersides are silvery-grey while their backs are dark grey with dark spotted patterns. Their heads are small in size with narrow snouts. Adults weigh 60 to 150 kilograms.

Lifespan

About 30 to 35 years.

Length

Adult females, 151 to 169 centimeters.

Adult males, 161 to 176 centimeters.

Diet

They feed on herrings, Pollock, cod, capelin, fish and mollusks.

ALASKAN HARE

Breeding

Breeding occurs between April to May. After a gestational period of 46 days, 4 to 8 young ones are born. At birth, they weigh about 100 grams and are fully covered with fur and their eyes are open. Their pelage is usually brown and some may have a white center stripe. They are nursed for 5 to 9 weeks and are weaned at around this time after which they become independent and drift away from their mothers.

Appearance

In summer, these hares have a white undercoat and a dusky brown coat that is grizzled with grey being darker on top of the head and white on the under parts. Their nose and mouth have buff or cinnamon hair and around their dark eyes are white rings. Their ears are dusky washed with grey and sort as compared to those of other hares. Their hind feet are large and are covered with fur. In winter, their coat is entirely white except the tips of ears which usually have black fur throughout the year. Adults weigh 3 to 7 kilograms.

Length

Adult body length, 0.5 to 0.7 meters. Tail length, 8 centimeters.

Diet

They feed on barks, roots, shoots, willow leaves, woody vegetation, berries, flowers and grasses.

NORTHERN FLYING SQUIRREL
Breeding

Breeding occurs between March and May. Following a gestational period of 37 to 42 days, 1 to 6 young ones are born. At birth, they weigh 5 to 6 grams and their eyes and ears are closed. Their eyes open when they are 31 days old. Parental care is solely the mother's responsibility. The young leave the nest when they are about 40 days old.

Weaning occurs when they are 2 months of age but they remain with their mothers until they are 3 months old after which they become independent.

Appearance

Northern flying squirrels have cinnamon brown to silky grey pelage and a fleshy membrane is present extending from their foreleg wrist to the hindleg ankle. They have a tail that is flattened and furred with a rounded end.

Their tails usually make up about eighty percent of their bodies. The eyes of northern flying squirrels are black. Both males and females resemble each other. Adults weigh about 75 to 140 grams.

Lifespan

Up to 4 years.

Length

Adult total body length, 275 to 342 millimeters.

Diet

They feed on nuts, fungi, acorn, nectar, fruits, buds, bird egg, insects, seeds and lichen.

GROUND HOG
Breeding

Breeding occurs from March to mid or late April. After a gestational period of 31 to 32 days, females give birth to one to nine young ones. Prior to giving birth, the female will prepare a nest using plant fibers inside a den. At birth, the young are blind, naked and helpless and females are the primary caregivers. Weaning occurs at around 5 to 6 weeks after which they become independent.

Appearance

 They are stocky with a dark reddish-brown to yellowish pelage that appears grizzled due to the light-coloured tips present on their hairs. Their bellies are straw-coloured and their feet are dark-brown to black. Their tail is usually bushy and short ranging in colour from dark-brown to black. The legs of ground hog are short and strong and their feet have claws. They possess rounded ears. Adults weigh 2 to 6 kilograms with males being larger than females.

Lifespan

About 3 to 10 years.

Length

Adult total body length, 41 to 68 centimeters.

Diet

They feed on mulberries, raspberries, grasshoppers, buckwheat, buttercup, timothy-grass, sheep sorrel, agrimony, clover, sheep sorrel and alfalfa.

PACIFIC WHITE-SIDED DOLPHIN

Breeding

Breeding occurs between August and October. Following a gestational period of 9 to 12 months, 1 young one is born. At birth the young weigh about 13 to 22 kilograms. Parental care is solely provided by the mother and males take no part in raising the young. The young are nursed for up to 18 months. Weaning starts when the young are 12 months old and lasts until they are 18 months old after which they become independent.

Appearance

They have a black to grey coloration with their sides having light-grey stripes, flippers and dorsal fin. These stripes start from the side of their faces and extend to the base of their tails. Their anterior and dorsal fins have light grey patch while their eyes and mouths are dark in appearance. Their tails and hooked bicolored dorsal fins are key distinguishing features. The bodies of these dolphins are robust and their beaks are short. Adults weigh 78 to 200 kilograms with males being larger than females.

Lifespan

About 40 years.

Length

Adult males, body length, 2.5 meters.

Adult females, body length, 2.3 meters.

Diet

They feed on sardines, pacific mackerel, capelin, herring, squid, anchovies and hake.

BEARDED SEAL

Breeding

Breeding occurs between March and June and after a gestational period of 11 months, females give birth to one young one. At birth, the young weigh 34 kilograms. Parental care is solely the female's responsibility. Weaning occurs when the young are 18 to 24 days old. Once weaning is complete, the young become independent.

Appearance

Adult bearded seals have a light grey to dark-brown coloration with their backs having a darker coloration than the rest of their bodies. Their faces and flippers have a deep rust to brick coloration. These seals have distinct moustaches with their front and hind flippers having pointed claws that are pronounced. Adults weigh 200 to 430 kilograms with females being larger than males.

Lifespan

Up to 25 years in the wild.

Length

Adult head to body length, 2.3 meters.

Diet

They feed on shrimps, clams, crabs, whelks, cod, sculpin, squid and fish.

AMERICAN BISON

Breeding

Breeding occurs from late June to September and after a gestational period of 274 days, one young one is born. At birth, the young weigh 15 to 25 kilograms and are red in color. They are usually fully developed at birth and parental care is solely offered by the females with males taking no part in raising the young. The young are nursed for about 7 to 8 months and are weaned when they are 7 to 12 months old. After weaning is complete, the young attain independence when they are one year old.

Appearance

The fur of American bison is brown in colour and varies from the front to the back. They have longer hair in front as compared to the back. American bisons also have black horns which curve upwards and inwards and end in a sharp tip. These animals also possess

a shoulder hump and a huge head. Adults weigh 318 to 900 kilograms with males being larger than females.

Lifespan

About 15 to 20 years in the wild.

Length

Adult males, head to body length, 3.6 to 3.8 meters.

Shoulder height, 1.67 to 1.86 meters.

Adult females head to body length, 2.13 to 3.18 meters.

Shoulder height, 1.52 to 1.57 meters.

Diet

They feed on leaves, wood, bark, stems and grasses.

ALASKA MARMOT

Breeding

Breeding occurs once yearly, in June. After a gestational period of 5 to 6 weeks, 3 to 18 young ones are born. Both parents provide parental care to the young. At birth, the young are helpless and by 6 weeks, they are weaned. The young then remain with their parents until they are 2 years old at which time they become independent.

Appearance

Alaska marmots have coarse hair that ranges in colour from black to brown to white. Their back usually has brown hair and they have a lighter brown coloration underneath their black-

tipped
guard hairs.
They are
heavy
bodies with
a short neck
and a
slightly
flattened

tail. On top of their heads there is black fur which extends to the neck from the tip of their noses. Their feet and lips are black and their front feet may have white markings. The legs of Alaska marmots are thick, muscular and short. They have small eyes and their ears are broad, short, furry and rounded. They possess cheek pouches. Alaska marmots usually moult once, during summer. Adults weigh 2.5 to 4 kilograms with males being larger than females.

Lifespan

About 13 to 15 years.

Length

Adult body length, 539 to 652 millimeters.

Diet

They feed on grasses, legumes, fruits, forbs, leaves, seeds, flowers, nuts, grains and leaves.

RIBBON SEAL
Breeding

Breeding occurs between May and June. After a gestational period of 10 to 11 months, one young one is born. At birth, the young weigh 6 to 10 kilograms and are 73 to 98 centimeters long. They are usually nursed and raised in packed ice for 4 to 6 weeks after which weaning occurs. Parental care is solely the female's responsibility. Once the nursing period is complete, the young are taught how to dive for food by their mothers after which they become independent.

Appearance

The bodies of these seals are cylindrical and their limbs are modified for swimming . As they mature, their body colour changes and adult males have a reddish-brown coloration which becomes black once they undergo moulting. Ribbon seals have four

white bands over their bodies thus creating a black and white pattern. One band is located around each fore flippers, one around each hind flippers, one around the lower back and one around the neck. The site where these bands are located varies between individuals and these markings are more distinct in males. Adults weigh 70 to 80 kilograms with males being larger than females.

Lifespan

About 20 to 30 years.

Length

Adult body length, 5 to 6 feet.

Diet

They feed on fish, cephalopods, crustaceans and mollusks.

COMMON DOLPHIN

Breeding

Mating occurs all year round with no specific mating season. After a gestational period of 10 to 12 months, females give birth to 1 to 3 young ones. Upon birth, the young are immediately part of the members of the family group. Parental care is solely the female's responsibility. The young nurse until they are 6 months old after which they are weaned. They continue to suckle until they are one and a half years old after which they become independent although there is usually post-independence association with parents.

Appearance

Common dolphins have a dark brown or black back with a cream or white underside. Stretching from their lower jaw to their flippers is a dark streak and their flippers and fluke s resemble the back in coloration and can be dark brown or black. On their sides are crisscross patterns that resemble an hourglass and which divide the bottom colours from the top colours. This band usually has a grey appearance towards the tail and a buff tan appearance in front. Adults weigh 100 to 136 kilograms and males are slightly larger than females.

Lifespan

About 35 to 40 years.

Length

Adult female body length, 2.6 meters.

Adult male body length, 2.7 meters.

Diet

They feed on herrings, pilchard, sardines, small bonito, sauries, squid, octopus, anchovies, nocturnal hake and mollusks.

WAPITI
Breeding

Breeding occurs in September to early October and following a gestational period of 240 to 262 days, 1 to 2 young ones are born. At birth, the young weigh 15 to 16 kilograms and are hidden by their mothers in secluded areas. Parental care is solely the female's responsibility and males play no part in caring for the young. Weaning occurs when the young are 2 months old. The young remain with their mothers for the first year of their lives after which they become independent.

Appearance

They range in colour from tan in summer to dark brown in winter and their rump is buff in colour. They have a darker coloration on their legs, bellies, heads and necks and their heads are long. They possess large ears and males have antlers that are wide and a dark mane that is shaggy hangs from their necks to their chests. The tail of wapiti is short. Adult males are larger than females and weigh

178 to 497 kilograms while females weigh 171 to 292 kilograms.

Lifespan

About 20 years.

Length

Adult male head to body length, 210 to 240 centimeters.

Shoulder height, 145 to 165 centimeters.

Adult female head to body length, 190 to 230 centimeters.

Shoulder height, 130 to 150 centimeters.

Tail length, 10 to 16 centimeters.

Diet

They feed on violets, clover, aster, hawkweed, dandelions, mushrooms, leaves, lichen, wood, bark, stems, root, tubers and fungus.

MOUNTAIN LION
Breeding

Breeding occurs between December and March and following a gestational period of 84 to 106 days, females give birth to 1 to 6 young ones. At birth, the young weigh about 226 to 453 grams and are deaf, helpless and blind. Their eyes open 10 days after birth and their ears also open around this time. Weaning occurs between 28 to 40 days. Parental care is solely the female's responsibility. The young then remain with their mothers for up to 26 months after weaning after which males will disperse 23 to 274 kilometers while females disperse 9 to 140 kilometers away from their natal territory.

Appearance

They are large cats with slender bodies and their coat ranges in colour from greyish brown to yellowish brown on its upper parts with the belly having a pale and buffy coloration. Their chests and throat have a white appearance. Their noses are pink and are bordered by a black line that extends to their lips. The area behind their ears, tip of tail and muzzle stripes have a black coloration while their eyes are golden to greyish brown. Mountain lions have long tails that are cylindrical and make up to a third of their total length. Adult males are larger than females weighing 36 to 120 kilograms while females weigh 29 to 64 kilograms.

Lifespan

In the wild, 18 to 20 years.

Length

Adult males head to body length, 1020 to 1540 millimeters. Tail length, 680 to 960 millimeters.

Adult females head to body length, 860 to 1310 millimeters. Tail length, 630 to 790 millimeters.

Shoulder height, 53 to 71 centimeters.

Diet

They feed on moose, mule deer, elk, muskrat, porcupine, beaver, raccoon, striped skunk, rabbits, coyotes, birds, bobcats, opossums, caribou and white-tailed deer.

NORTHERN ELEPHANT SEAL
Breeding

Breeding occurs between December and January. After a gestational period of 11 months, a single young one is born. Parental care is solely the female's responsibility. When the young are around 23 to 27 days old, they are weaned after which the mother leaves the young one and returns to the sea. The young ones who have been left form groups that are known as pods and remain on the shore for up to 12 weeks. During this time, they no longer receive parental care.

Appearance

They are bar skinned and have a black coloration prior to moulting. Upon moulting, they usually have a dark grey to silver coat which fades to tan and brownish-yellow. The necks and chests of adult males are hairless and have pink, white and light brown speckles. The eyes of northern elephant seal are round, large and black. They possess pectoral fins and their hind limbs are atrophied with underdeveloped ends which form the tail fin and tail. Juveniles are usually black at birth and become silver-grey following weaning. Adult males are larger in size than females and weigh 1500 to 2300 kilograms while females weigh 400 to 900 kilograms.

Lifespan

Females, about 19 years.

Males, about 13 years.

Length

Adult male total body length, 4 to 5 meters.

Adult females total body length, 2.5 to 3.6 meters.

Diet

They feed on squids, fishes, sharks and rays.

FISHER
Breeding

Breeding occurs in late winter and early spring between March and May. After a gestational period of 11 to 12 months, females give birth to 1 to 6 young ones. At birth, the young are almost hairless and blind weighing around 40 grams. When they are 53 days old, they open their eyes. Females are solely responsible for caring for the young with no help from males. Weaning occurs when the young are 8 to 16 weeks old. When the young attain 5 months, they become independent.

Appearance

The coat of fishers ranges in colour from medium to dark brown with their heads and shoulders having gold or silver hoariness and their legs and tails having a black coloration. a cream chest patch may also be present which varies in shape and size between individuals. Adult males are noticeably larger than females weighing around 3500 to 5000 grams while females weigh 2000 to 2500 grams.

Lifespan

In the wild, up to 10 years.

Length

Adult males, 900 to 1200 millimeters. Tail length, 370 to 410 millimeters.

Adult females, 750 to 950 millimeters. Tail length, 310 to 360 millimeters.

Shoulder height, 30 to 45 centimeters.

Diet

They feed on snowshoe hares, squirrels, porcupines, mice, birds, shrews, fruits and berries.

BLUE WHALE
Breeding

Breeding occurs in late fall and winter. After a gestational period of 10 to 12 months,

females give birth to a single calf. At birth, calves are around 7.6 meters long and weight up to 2250 kilograms. Parental care is solely the females responsibility with males playing no part in caring for the young. The young nurse up to 6 months and weaning occurs when they are 6 to 8 months old and remain

with their mothers until they are 2 to 3 years old after which they become independent.

Appearance

These whales have slender bodies with a U-shaped head that is broad. Their flippers are elongated and thin. They have a dorsal fin that is sickle shaped and is located close to their tails. Their skin has a greyish-blue coloration that is mottled and when they are underwater, it appears blue. A lighter pigmentation is present on their underbellies and at times their underbelly appears yellowish. Adult males weigh up to 100 metric tons while females weigh up to 112 metric tons.

Lifespan

About 80 to 90 years.

Length

Adult total body length, 75 to 80 feet.

Diet

They mainly feed on krill but also eat small fish, small crustaceans, squid, zooplankton and copepods.

SHORT-FINNED PILOT WHALE

Breeding

Breeding occurs all year round with a peak between July and August. After a gestational period of 15 months, one young one is born. Females are solely responsible for caring for the young and males play no role in raising their offspring. Females are usually helped by other females of the pod to raise the young. Weaning occurs when the young are 2 years old. Independence is attained at 3 years with the males leaving their mothers while the females continue living in the pod with their mothers.

Appearance

They are black in colour with grey-white markings on their chests and throats resembling an elongated anchor. Around their dorsal fin is a grey saddle and their heads have a bulging forehead. Their snout is slender and beak-like and their flippers are pointed. Adults weigh about 4000 kilograms with males being larger than females.

Lifespan

About 45 to 60 years.

Length

Adult male total body length, 5 to 6 meters.

Adult female, total body length, 4 to 5 meters.

Diet

They feed on squid, octopus, fish and mollusks.

BIRDS

BALD EAGLE
Breeding

Breeding occurs mid-September to January. Females then lay 1 to 3 whitish eggs that are oval. These are incubated for around

35 days. Both males and females take part in brooding the eggs with females brooding more frequently as compared to males. Upon hatching, the young weigh about 60 grams. They are usually brooded constantly by both parents and males provide most of the food to them within the first two weeks. When they are 8 to 14 days old, they undergo fledging but may remain

with their parents until they are 18 weeks after which they become independent.

Appearance

Adults are large in size with yellow coloration on their beaks and eyes. Their bodies are dark brown to black while their heads and tails are white in colour. Juveniles usually have dark eyes and pink legs upon hatching and in their first year their eyes, beaks and bodies are dark brown. Their eyes usually lighten to greyish brown as they mature and eventually their eyes and beaks become yellow. The feathers on their heads also lighten. When they are about five years old, they attain the adult plumage. Adults possess large necks, bills and heads and the talons on their feet are sharp. They weigh about 4.3 kilograms with males being smaller than females.

Lifespan

In the wild, 15 to 20 years.

Length

Adult body length, 79 to 94 centimeters.

Wingspan, 178 to 229 centimeters.

Diet

They feed on rainbow trout, gizzard shads, American eels, kokanee salmon, chum salmon, snow geese, ross geese, common murres, tundra swans, auklets, ground squirrels, Norway rats, montane voles, birds and carrion.

SHORT-BILLED GULL
Breeding

Breeding occurs between March and April. Females lay 3 to 5 eggs that are incubated by both males and females. These hatch after 25 days. Once chicks hatch, both parents care for them and by the 20th day, they are capable of foraging by themselves. At around 35 days, they fledge but remain with their parents until around 8 weeks of age after which they become independent.

Appearance

The head of short-billed gull is white and its bill is greenish-yellow. Their wings and backs are grey. The young usually have a brown coloration with tan spots and their beak is dark in colour. The legs of short-billed gulls are yellowish-green and their feet are webbed. Adults weigh about 290 to 552 grams with males being larger than females.

Lifespan

In the wild, up to 24 years.

Length

Adult body length, 40 to 45 centimeters.

Wingspan, 100 to 120 centimeters.

Diet

They feed on worms, insects, berries, mice, herring, cod, grains, clams, mussels, crustaceans and young sea birds.

COMMON RAVEN
Breeding

Breeding occurs around mid-February to May and females lay 3 to 7 eggs which are incubated for 20 to 25 days. Incubation is solely done by females. Once the eggs hatch, both parents take part in caring for the young. The young are capable of leaving the nest when they are 5 to 7 days weeks old and attain independence at this time.

Appearance

They are black in colour and their tail is wedge-shaped. On their throats, there is a ruff of feathers known as hackles. The base of their neck feathers has a pale brownish-grey colouration. Present above their beaks are shaggy feathers. The bill of common raven is black and robust in size and they possess a dark brown iris. Adults weigh 689 to 1625 grams.

Lifespan

In the wild, about 13 years.

Length

Adult body length, 54 to 67 centimeters.

Wingspan, 115 to 150 centimeters.

Diet

They feed on maggots, carrion beetles, berries, grains, fruit, birds, fish, figs and cranberries.

GLAUCOUS-WINGED GULL

Breeding

Breeding occurs in summer. Females lay 2 to 3 eggs that are yellow-green in colour with blotches of brown and grey. Both males and females incubate the eggs for 26 to 29 days. Upon hatching, the young are covered in down and are capable of leaving the nest within 2 days of hatching. Parental care is provided by both males and females. Fledging occurs at 37 to 53 days after which the young become independent around 2 weeks later.

Appearance

The head, neck, breast, belly and tail of glaucous winged gull are white while their wings are silver-grey. They have grey wingtips and a mantle resembling the wingtips in colour. Their beaks are yellow with a red spot near the end. The iris of glaucous-winged gull is dark and is surrounded by pale skin. In winter, they develop a darker colouration on their heads and nape with a mottled pattern and their bills become duller in colour with a dark marking at the tip. Juveniles range in colour from brown to  grey and their beaks are black. Adults weigh 730 to 1690 grams.

Lifespan

About 15 years.

Length

Adult body length, 50 to 68 centimeters.

Adult wingspan, 120 to 150 centimeters.

Diet

They feed on fish, chitons, clams, mussels, barnacles, sea urchins, eggs, small birds and limpets.

AMERICAN ROBIN
Breeding

Breeding occurs between April to July. Females then lay 3 to 5 eggs in a nest that can be located on the ground or on a tree. Egg incubation is done by females and they hatch after 14 days. Both males and females take part in caring for the young. The female broods the young and feeds them. 2 weeks after hatching, fledging (leaving the nest) occurs. Two weeks after fledging, the young become independent.

Appearance

American robins have brown backs and reddish colouration on their breast. Their lower belly and under tail feathers are white and their throats are white with a black streak. Present above and below their eyes are white crescents. Females have a slightly lighter plumage as compared to males. On the breasts of juveniles, there are dark spots. Juveniles also appear paler as compared to adult males. Adults weigh around 77 grams.

Lifespan

About 2 years.

Length

Adult body length, 23 to 28 centimeters.

Wingspan, 119 to 137 millimeters.

Diet

They feed on beetles, caterpillars, grasshoppers, fruits, earthworms and berries.

BLACK-BILLED MAGPIE
Breeding

Breeding occurs from late March to early June. Females lay 6 to 9 greenish-grey eggs that have brown markings. After an incubation period of 25 days, the eggs hatch. Females solely incubate eggs while males feed them. Upon hatching, chicks are featherless and their eyes are closed. Both males and females take part in caring for the young. They fledge at around 24 to 30 days and become independent at 70 days.

Appearance

Black-bellied magpies have black colouration on their heads, upper breasts, tails and backs and their wings and lower breasts have white patches. Their bills are heavy and black and their legs are black. On their tails, bodies and wings, they usually have iridescent patches which can be bronze to green in colour. Adults weigh

145 to 210 grams with males being larger than females.

Lifespan

About 4 to 6 years.

Length

Adult body length, 45 to 60 centimeters.

Wingspan, 175 to 210 millimeters.

Diet

They feed on insects, seeds, berries, rodents, nuts, eggs and carrion.

MALLARD
Breeding

Breeding occurs between October to March. Females lay 9 to 13 creamy to greyish eggs which are incubated for 26 to 28 days. Nests are usually located on the ground near water bodies. Females solely incubate the eggs. Upon hatching, the young are alert and are covered in down. The female leads them to water and they abandon the nest.

Appearance

They are medium-sized birds and during the breeding season, males usually have a glossy head with bottle-green coloration. A white collar demarcating the purple tinged brown breast from the head is also present. On the rear, they have a black colouration with dark tail feathers that are bordered by white. Their bill is usually yellowish-orange with a black tip. Females range from buff to dark brown in colour with buff eyebrows, cheeks, throat and neck, a darker eye stripe and crown and a black to mottled orange and brown bill. Adults weigh 0.7 to 1.6 kilograms.

Lifespan

About 5 to 10 years.

Length

Adult body length, 50 to 65 centimeters.

Wingspan, 81 to 98 centimeters.

Diet

They feed on worms, insects, gastropods, arthropods.

BLACK-LEGGED KITTIWAKE
Breeding

Breeding occurs between April to August. Females lay 1 to 3 eggs which are incubated by both males and females for up to 27 days. Once the chicks hatch, both males and females take part in caring for them. At 40 days of age, the chicks fledge after which they become independent.

Appearance

They are small-sized with pearl grey wings and backs and their undersides and heads are white. They have a black colouration on the tips of their tail feathers. The bill of adults has a greenish-yellow appearance. The legs of black-legged kittiwake are mostly black but can be red or orange. Adults weigh around 317 grams.

Lifespan

About 10 years.

Length

Adult body length, 37 to 41 centimeters.

Wingspan, 91 to 105 centimeters.

Diet

They feed on capelin, arctic cod, saffron cod, Pollock, small trout and young salmon.

DARK-EYED JUNCO
Breeding

Breeding occurs in April. Females then construct nests where they lay 3 to 6 pale green to white eggs that have brown spots. After an incubation period of 12 to 13 days, the eggs hatch. Females solely incubate the eggs but males and females provide care to the young and protect them. Upon hatching, chicks are helpless and the

female broods them. They begin growing feathers when they

are seven days old. At around 9 to 13 days, the young leave the nest but are still dependent on their parents until they are 9 to 21 days old after which they become independent.

Appearance

The plumage of dark-eyed junco is dark grey on the head, upper parts and breast while its outer tail and belly are white in colour. The white colouration of the feathers of their outer tail is usually more distinct in flight. Juveniles and females have a browner appearance. The breast of juveniles is streaked and their beaks have yellowish edges. The bill of adult dark-eyed junco is pink. Adults weigh around 19 grams with males being larger than females.

Lifespan

About 3 to 11 years.

Length

Adult body length, 12 to 16 centimeters.

Diet

They feed on seeds, grains, crab grass, dropseed grass, pigweed, goosefoot, ragweed, bristle grass and pigweed.

AMERICAN WIGEON

Breeding

Breeding occurs in spring. Females lay 6 to 12 eggs that have a creamy white colouration. These are incubated solely by the female for 37 to 48 days. Upon hatching, the hatchlings are able to leave the nest with the female. The chicks become independent at around 37 to 48 days.

Appearance

During the non-breeding season, females usually have grey or brown plumage while males resemble the females with both having pale blue bills that have black tips. The bellies of both males and females are white and their legs and feet are grey. During the breeding season, males have green feathers around their eyes and running from the crown of their heads to their bills they have cream-coloured caps. They also possess white bellies. When on flight, a white shoulder patch is visible on their wings. Adults weigh 512 to 330 grams.

Lifespan

About 2 to 21 years.

Length

Adult body length, 42 to 59 centimeters.

Wingspan, 76 to 91 centimeters.

Diet

They feed on pondweeds, sedges, wild celery, algae, eelgrass, snails and insects.

COMMON MERGANSER

Breeding

Breeding occurs once yearly, between May to June. Females then lay 6 to 17 pale yellow to white buff appearance. After an incubation of 28 to 35 days, the eggs hatch. Upon hatching, the young are fully developed and are capable of leaving the nest within 48 hours. They are then led by the female to feeding sites where the young find food for themselves. Parental care is solely the female's responsibility and males do not take part in raising the young. The young become independent at around 30 to 50 days and fledging occurs at around 60 to 85 days.

Appearance

Female common mergansers have a brown colouration on their heads while their bodies have a mixture of white and gr and their breast is white. A line is present between their white breast and brown necks. Males usually have a black back, black to dark green heads which are brown during the breeding season. They possess red feet and bills and their bills are serrated. Their bodies are white and a tinge of peach is present on their breast. Adults weigh 1050 to 2054 grams with males being larger than females.

Lifespan

About 12 years.

Length

Adult body length, 53 to 69 centimeters

Wingspan, 86 to 99 centimeters.

Diet

They feed on frogs, fish, mollusks, snails and marine worms.

COMMON MURRE
Breeding

Breeding occurs between March and July. Females then lay one white to blue egg with brown or black speckles. The egg is incubated by both the male and female for 28 to 34 days. At around 20 days of age, the chick leaves the nest and goes to the water. Both parents care for the chicks. At about 18 to 25 days of age, the chick goes to the sea with the male. The chick is capable of flight at 39 to 46 days.

Appearance

 During the breeding season, adults have a dark brown colouration on their heads, backs and necks and their underbelly is white in colour. Their secondary feathers have white tips. The feet and legs of these birds are dark greyish-black while their bills are dark and slender. In winter, they have a dark spur that extends from the back of their eye and white colouration on the cheeks and throat. Juveniles resemble adults but have darker heads. Adults weigh 945 to 1044 grams.

Lifespan

About 20 to 26 years.

Length

Adult body length, 38 to 46 centimeters.

Wingspan, 61 to 73 centimeters.

Diet

They feed on marine worms, squid, amphipods, mollusks and crustaceans.

SANDHILL CRANE

Breeding

Breeding occurs between December and August. Both males

and females
take part in
constructing
the nest after
which the
female lays 1
to 3 oval
shaped eggs
that are brown
and have

reddish spots. The eggs are incubated by both males and females. Following an incubation period of 29 to 32 days, the eggs hatch. Both parents provide care to the young and feed them. The chicks usually stay with their parents until they are 9 to 10 months old and then they become independent.

Appearance

They have an overall grey colouration with long necks and legs and a bright red patch on their heads and white patches on their cheeks. Their beaks are long and pointed and are dark grey in colour. Juveniles have sandy brown appearance. Adults weigh 3 to 5 kilograms with males being larger than females.

Lifespan

About 21 years.

Length

Adult height, 80 to 122 centimeters.

Wingspan, 2 meters.

Diet

They feed on seeds, grains, fruit, nuts, berries, snails, mollusks, rats, quails, mice and insects.

WHITE-CROWNED SPARROW

Breeding

Breeding occurs in spring. Females construct a nest where they lay 3 to 5 eggs that are grey or greenish blue with brown marks. These are incubated for 11 to 14 days by the female. Upon hatching, the chicks are helpless and blind and both parents provide care for the young. When the chicks are 8 to 10 days old, they leave the nest.

Appearance

Males and females have black stripes extending along the crown of their heads and behind their eyes. These stripes outline the solid white feathers on their heads. The breast of white-crowned sparrow is light grey and their flight feathers are dark brown.

Their coverts have white banded tips. The young usually have a browner colouration with their heads having brown stripes that surround their darker white patch. Adults weigh about 25 grams.

Lifespan

About 13 years.

Length

Adult body length, 18 centimeters.

Wingspan, 21 to 24 centimeters.

Diet

They feed on buds, flowers, berries, caterpillars, wasps, spiders, beetles and grasses.

ARCTIC TERN
Breeding

Breeding occurs between June and July. Females then lay 2 to 3

 eggs which are incubated for 21 to 22 days. Upon hatching, the chicks are capable of moving around within 3 days. Both males and females care for the young and protect them especially in the first ten days of life. The young are capable of flying at around 10 to 15 days and they become independent when they are 20 to 35 days old.

Appearance

Adults have a grey colouration with a black colouration on the crown and nape and a white colouration on the cheeks. They are pale grey on their upper wings and have a translucent area near their wingtip. They have white tails with pale grey under parts. In winter, their crowns are white and their bills darker.

The bills and legs of juveniles are black with a white fore crown. Adults weigh 86 to 127 grams.

Lifespan

About 30 years.

Length

Adult body length, 33 to 36 centimeters.

Wingspan, 76 centimeters.

Diet

They feed on crayfish, sand eels, capelins, sand launaes.

TRUMPETER SWAN
Breeding

Breeding occurs between March to May. Both males and

females take part in constructing the nest. Females then lay 4 to 6 eggs which hatch within 32 to 37 days. These birds usually incubate their eggs using their feet. Once the eggs hatch, the young are fully developed and are capable of swimming within 24 hours of hatching. Both parents take part in caring for the young. Fledging occurs at around 91 to 119 days and at around one year, the young become independent.

Appearance

Adults have completely white feathers but some may have a grey-white colouration. The feet, tarsals and bill of trumpeter swans are black while their bills have a small pink line that can be red. Juveniles have a light to dark grey colouration on their bodies that becomes whiter as they mature. Their feet are usually grey yellow in colour and their bills have a black base and a pink colouration. Adults weigh 9.5 to 13.5 kilograms.

Lifespan

About 25 years.

Length

Adult body length, 1.4 to 1.6 meters.

Wingspan, 2 to 2.4 meters.

Diet

They feed on leaves, roots, duck potato, water weeds, pond weeds, sago weed, horsetail and marine worms.

WILLOW PTARMIGAN

Breeding

Breeding occurs in spring and summer months once yearly. Females lay 4 to 14 eggs that are incubated for 20 to 23 days. Females solely incubate the eggs while the male protects the female during this period. Upon hatching, the young are fully developed and weigh around 15 grams. They are capable of leaving the nest upon hatching. Both males and females take part in caring for the young. They fledge

when they are 10 to 12 days and attain independence at 5 to 7 months of age.

Appearance

During spring, females usually have a mottled brown and ochre appearance and males develop a chestnut colouration with dark brown barring on their bodies and tails. Present on their eyes are red combs. In fall, adults adopt a lighter colouration with males retaining their dark barring pattern and adopting ochre colouration while females become white or grey. Adults weigh 430 to 810 grams with males being larger than females.

Lifespan

About 9 years.

Length

Adult body length, 280 to 432 millimeters.

Wingspan, 61 centimeters.

Diet

They feed on leaves, wood, seeds, grains, fruit, nuts, flowers, caterpillars and beetles.

RED-NECKED GREBE
Breeding

Breeding occurs between May to September. Both males and females take part in building the nest. Females then lay 1 to 9 light blue eggs that are incubated by both males and females for 22 to 35 days. Once all chicks have hatched, they leave the nest. The chicks often ride on their parents back until around 10 to 17 days after which they begin swimming. Both parents care for the young and at around 9 to 10 weeks, the young fledge. They become independent thereafter.

Appearance

In winter, their heads have black tops and grey sides with a white crescent that spans to the lower lateral sides of their heads from their throats. On the anterior part of their necks, they are white or light grey. On the rest of their bodies, they have a dark colouration. A distinct pale grey patch develops on the sides of their heads in summer but the rest of their plumage is similar to that of the non-breeding season. The bills of these birds are usually black with the base of the upper and lower mandible having an orange-yellow colouration. Their eyes have a dark brown iris with a yellow ring around it. Adult weigh 800 to 1600 grams with males being larger than females.

Lifespan

About 5 years.

Length

Adult body length, 46 to 52 centimeters.

Wingspan, 60 to 85 centimeters.

Diet

They feed on small fish, tadpoles, salamanders, crayfish, crustaceans and aquatic insects.

CANADA GOOSE

Breeding

Breeding occurs once yearly, from April to May. Females build nests where they lay 2 to 10 eggs. Females incubate the eggs for 28 to 30 days after which the eggs hatch. Upon hatching, the young are capable of leaving the nest within 24 hours and their parents lead them to find food and water. Both parents provide care for the young. Fledging occurs between 40 to 48 days but the young remain with their parents until they are a year old after which they become independent.

Appearance

The plumage of Canada geese has feathers that are brown-grey on the dorsal region and cream-white on the rump and belly. Their heads and necks are long and black while their beaks have a distinct white mark close to the chin. Juveniles have a yellow colouration with grey-green feathers on their heads and dorsum. Their feet are usually black. Adults weigh around 3 to 10 kilograms with males being larger than females.

Lifespan

About 10 to 24 years.

Length

Adult body length, 76 to 110 centimeters.

Wingspan, 1.3 to 1.7 meters.

Diet

They feed on leaves, grass, berries, seed, algae, mollusks, grains and nuts.

AMERICAN CROW

Breeding

Breeding occurs in. both males and females take part in building the nest. The female then lays 3 to 8 eggs that are light green with brown speckles. These are incubated by the female and hatch within 18 days. During the incubation period, the male feeds the female. Upon hatching, both parents provide care to the young with assistance from helpers. At around 28 to 35 days, the chicks fledge after which they become independent.

Appearance

Adults have black feathers that are glossy with a slight iridescent look. They possess black bills that are slightly hooked on the end. The toes and legs of American crow are strong. The young can have brown wing and tail feathers that become glossy once they undergo their first moult. Their eyes are blue and a pink colouration is present inside their mouths. Adults weigh around 450 grams with males being larger than females.

Lifespan

About 14 years.

Length

Adult body length, 40 to 50 centimeters.

Wingspan, 85 to 100 centimeters.

Diet

They feed on worms, insects, insect larvae, fruits, nuts, grains, frogs, young rabbits, mice, eggs, mollusks and carrion.

HORNED PUFFIN

Breeding

Breeding occurs from April to July. Females lay one oval shaped grey egg with purple dots. The egg hatches after an incubation period of about 41 days. Both males and females take turns to incubate the egg. Upon hatching, the chick is helpless and both parents provide care to the young for up to one week. The chick remains in the nest for 37 to 46 days and fledging occurs at around 34 to 40 days and the chicks become independent thereafter.

Appearance

During the breeding season, adults have a black plumage and their faces are white with a yellow bill that has an orange-tip. The breast and belly is white and their legs and feet have a vivid orange colouration. Extending above the eyes are fleshy horns. Extending towards the back from the eye is a dark eye stripe. During the non-breeding season, their faces are soot grey and their bills have a greyish base. Juveniles possess purely grey bills that are triangular in shape. Their feet range in colour from pink to grey. Adults weigh around 500 grams.

Lifespan

Up to 20 years.

Length

Adult body length, 32 centimeters.

Wingspan, 185 to 199 millimeters.

Diet

They feed on herrings, capelin, salmon, cod, marine worms, squid, sand lances and mollusks.

HARLEQUIN DUCK
Breeding

Breeding occurs between May and June. Females lay 5 to 8 eggs which are incubated solely by the female and during this period, the male migrates to the ocean to undergo moulting. The incubation period is 27 to 29 days after which the eggs hatch. Upon hatching, the female takes the young to the water where she teaches them how to find food for themselves. When the young are 60 to 70 days old, they start flying. Parental care is solely the female's responsibility and the young become independent at around 70 days. Once the young are independent, there can still be post-independence association with the parents.

Appearance

The bodies of male harlequin-ducks are blue-grey with white patches on the head and body that are distinct. Their flanks are chestnut in colour. The white patches on their heads and bodies are outlined with black. Females have a dusky brown appearance and on each side of their faces, they possess two to three whitish patches. When in flight, males exhibit white colouration on their wings and a metallic blue speculum is also present but these are absent in females. Adults weigh 0.45 to 0.68 kilograms.

Lifespan

About 12 to 14 years.

Length

Adult body length, 35 to 50 centimeters.

Wingspan, 61 to 70 centimeters.

Diet

They feed on crustaceans, fish, eggs, mollusks, insects, limpets, chitons, mussels, amphipods and small clams.

BLACK-CAPPED CHICKADEE

Breeding

Breeding occurs between April to early August. Both males and females take part in constructing the nest. The female then lays 5 to 10 eggs. Incubation is solely done by females and lasts for 12 to 13 days and during this period, the male feeds the female. Upon hatching, the chicks are helpless and both males and females take part in providing care to the young. Once the chicks are 14 to 18 days old, they fledge after which the male, female and the chicks leave the nest and travel together. The young become independent at 5 to 6 weeks.

Appearance

The bodies of black-capped chickadees are short and plump and their backs and wings have a greenish-grey colouration with streaks of white and black on the wing feathers. Their bellies have a white colouration with light red on the flanks. They possess a black cap and bib and their cheeks are white. The beaks of black-capped chickadees are pointed and black and their legs are dark. The young have a similar plumage to that of adults but their flanks have a more reddish colouration. Adults weigh about 11 grams.

Lifespan

About 2 years.

Length

Adult body length, 13 centimeters.

Wingspan, 20 millimeters.

Diet

They feed on seeds, berries, spiders, snails, caterpillars, insect eggs, insect larvae, sawflies and carrion.

TUFTED PUFFIN
Breeding

Breeding occurs between April to May. Females then lay one off-white to faint blue egg. Both males and females take turns in incubating the egg for 40 to 53 days. Upon hatching, both parents care for the chick and fledging occurs at 45 to 55 days after which the chick becomes independent.

Appearance

In preparation for spring breeding, tufted puffins usually have brownish-black bodies and on the underside of their wings, there are white feathers. Their faces are usually white and above and behind their eyes are yellow plumes. Their bill usually has yellow or green markings and is bright red in colour. In early summer, towards the end of the breeding season, they lose their plumes and their bill adopts a dull reddish-brown colouration. Their bellies are usually speckled with pale brown flecks. The feet and legs of tufted puffins vary from red to orange in colour.

Adults weigh 700 to 840 grams with males being larger than females.

Lifespan

About 20 years.

Length

Adult body length, 36 to 40 centimeters.

Wingspan, 74 centimeters.

Diet

They feed on octopuses, jellyfish, crabs, squids, zooplankton, cephalopods, crustaceans and mollusks.

SONG SPARROW

Breeding

Breeding occurs between April and August. Females build a nest where they lay 3 to 5 light greenish-blue eggs that are oval in shape and have a spotted appearance. These are incubated solely by the female fir 12 to 14 days after which they hatch. Both males and females provide care to the young who are usually helpless. At around 3 to 4 days of age, the young open

their eyes and are capable of flying when they are 17 days old. They become independent at around 18 to 20 days.

Appearance

Their plumage is heavily streaked with dark streaks which form a central chest spot. Their heads have a brown colouration and they possess a white or grey eye stripe and crown stripe. Their tails have brown-red coloured feathers and are rounded and quite long. The bill of song sparrows is usually dark brown. Adults weigh around 19 grams.

Lifespan

About 11 years.

Length

Adult body length, 12 to 17 centimeters.

Wingspan, 7 to 10 inches.

Diet

They feed on seeds, insects, fruits, arthropods, earthworms, caterpillars and insect larvae.

SAVANNAH SPARROW

Breeding

Breeding occurs between June to August. Females lay 2 to 6 eggs which are incubated for 10 to 13 days solely by the female. Upon hatching, the chicks are helpless and are dependent on their parents for care. Both parents show parental investment in their young ones. The chicks remain in the nest for around 8 to 11 days after which they fledge. Once fledging has occurred, both males and females continue caring for the young until they are 4 to 5 weeks old at which time they become independent.

Appearance

These birds are small in size and their backs are brown and dark streaked. Their under parts are whitish with their breast and flanks having brown or black streaks. They also possess whitish crown and supercilium stripes which can be yellow and their throats are white while their cheeks are brown in colour. Savannah sparrows possess dark eyes and horn-coloured legs and feet. The upper part of their bill is dark grey in colour while the lower part is horn-coloured. Adults weigh 15 to 29 grams.

Lifespan

About 6 years.

Length

Adult body length, 11 to 17 centimeters.

Wingspan, 18 to 25 centimeters.

Diet

They feed on beetles, grasshoppers, caterpillars, flies, spiders, fruits and seeds.

COMMON REDPOLL

Breeding

Breeding usually occurs from late April to August. Females lay 4 to 5 pale green eggs that have reddish brown spots. They solely incubate the eggs for around 10 to 11 days and during this period, the male feeds the female. Upon hatching, chicks are naked and helpless and both males and females take part in caring for them. At around 12 days, the young leave the nest and are independent by the 26th day of life.

Appearance

They have a brownish-grey plumage that is streaked with dark streaks and a bright red patch is present on their foreheads. Present on the wings of common redpoll are two pale stripes and a black bib. The breasts of male birds are suffused with red. Across their vent is a broad dark brown streak and their rump is also streaked. The legs of these birds are brown and their bills are yellowish and dark-tipped. They also possess dark brown irises.

Lifespan

About 2 to 3 years.

Length

Adult body length, 11 to 14 centimeters.

Wingspan, 19 to 22 centimeters.

Diet

They feed on grasses, sedges, berries, wildflowers insects and spiders.

GREATER YELLOWLEGS

Breeding

Breeding occurs between April and June. Their nests are usually located on the ground close to water. Females lay 3 to 5 buff coloured eggs that are marked with brown. These are incubated by both males and females for around 23 days. Soon after hatching, the young are capable of leaving the nest and searching for food. Both parents care for the young and fledging occurs at around 18 to 20 days. At about 35 to 40 days, the young become independent.

Appearance

 These birds are medium sized with a mottled brownish-grey pelage on their upper bodies that usually has pale spots.

Their under parts have a pale appearance. During the breeding season, they develop heavy dark streaks on their heads and necks and their flanks and upper chest are usually barred. The iris of greater yellowlegs is dark brown and when in flight, their legs extend beyond their tails. The young resemble adults but are more spotted above and their white breast possesses dark streaks. Adults weigh 111 to 187 grams.

Lifespan

Unknown.

Length

Adult body length, 14 inches.

Wingspan, 28 inches.

Diet

They feed on small fish, seeds, berries and frogs.

COMMON LOON

Breeding occurs in spring. Females lay 1 to 2 olive eggs that have brown or black spots. Both males and females incubate the eggs for around 24 to 31 days after which the eggs hatch. Upon hatching, the chicks are capable of swimming and diving underwater within 2 to 3 days. Both parents provide care to the young. At around 10 to 11 days, the young are able to fly and become independent when they are 2 to 3 months old.

Appearance

Their plumage is usually white, black and grey. In the breeding season, their heads are usually black and a white and black striped necklace is present around their necks. On their backs, they usually have a checkered pattern. In winter, their plumage is evenly grey on the back and head and their underside and neck a have a white colouration. The bill of common loon is black. The young usually have a plumage that is similar to the winter plumage of adults but their heads and backs have more white colouration. Adults weigh 1600 to 1800 grams with males being larger than females.

Lifespan

About 9 years.

Length

Adult body length, 70 to 90 centimeters.

Wingspan, 152 centimeters.

Diet

They feed on terrestrial worms, fish, insects, shrimp rock cod, gizzard shad, suckers, perch and minnows.

PELAGIC CORMORANT

Breeding

Breeding occurs between May and July. Females then lay 3 to 5 bluish-white eggs that are incubated by the female for around one month. Upon hatching, both males and females take part in caring for the young. When the chicks are 35 to 40 days old, they start making short flights. They are able to leave the nest at 45 to 55 days of life but remain dependent on their parents for food for a few more weeks after which they become independent.

Appearance

These birds have black plumage with glossy iridescent green bodies that have violet-purple or violet-bronze colouration on the neck. Their breeding plumage bears white patches on the flanks and at the base of the bill, they have red skin. They also possess two head crests and on their necks and upper-backs they have long white feathers. Adults weigh 1474 to 2438 grams.

Lifespan

About 18 years.

Length

Adult body length, 64 to 89 grams.

Wingspan 1 to 1.2 meters.

Diet

They feed on marine worms, algae, amphipods, fish, crustaceans, herrings, sand lance, shrimps, crabs and sculpins.

STELLER'S JAY
Breeding

Breeding occurs between late March to early July with a peak between April to May. Females lay 2 to 6 oval shaped eggs that have a glossy surface. Females solely incubate the eggs for around 16 days and are fed by the males during this period. Upon hatching, the chicks are helpless, naked and blind. Both parents care for the young. At around 18 days, they begin flying but remain with their parents until they are 6 to 7 weeks old at which time they become independent.

Appearance

The colour of their heads varies from blackish-brown to dark blue to black and on their foreheads, there are lighter streaks. They have a blue colouration beginning from their necks downwards while most of their body usually has a cobalt or dark blue colouration including their wings and retrices. Their beaks and feet have a black colouration with the beak being thick and pointed. They possess a distinct tall head crest that is black in colour. Juveniles are darker and can have brownish or greyish colouration on their upper parts and a duller colouration below. They usually have a sooty grey colouration on their heads and bodies and a shorter crest is present on their heads. Their blue portion is not as bright as that of adults. Adults weigh 100 to 140 grams.

Lifespan

About 16 years.

Length

Adult body length, 30 to 34 centimeters.

Wingspan, 45 to 48 centimeters.

Diet

They feed on seeds, nuts, fruits, berries, small rodents, eggs, lizards and snakes.

REPTILES

COMMON WATERSNAKE

Breeding

Breeding occurs between April and June and following a gestational period of 3 to 5 months, 4 to 99 young ones are born. Upon birth, the young are immediately independent and receive no parental care whatsoever. They are usually capable of finding food for themselves.

Appearance

They are dark-colored snakes with their color ranging from tan to brownish to greyish. Present on their backs and sides are several square blotches that alternate and merge to form bands. Mature snakes range in color from brown to black. The belly of common water snake ranges in colour from white to orange with half-moon shaped back edges to yellow. The young are usually reddish brown with a background coloration that can be brown, tan or grey. Adults weigh 81 to 408 grams.

Lifespan

About 9 years.

Length

Adult body length, 61 to 140 centimeters.

Diet

They feed on tadpoles, fish, leeches, large insects, birds, white-footed mice and carrion.

GREEN SEA TURTLE
Breeding

Breeding occurs in late spring. Females then lay up to 110 eggs in each nest. The eggs are usually incubated in warm sand and following a period of 2 months, the eggs hatch. Upon hatching,

the young find their way into the water. The young receive no parental care.

Appearance

Green sea turtles are large in size as compared to other hard – shelled sea turtles and possess a shell that ranges in color from grey to dark brown to olive with their underside being yellow-to-white in color. Five scutes run down the middle of their shells while four scutes are located on each side. Their beaks are serrated and present between their eyes are two large scales. Adults weigh 136 to 159 kilograms.

Lifespan

About 70 years.

Length

Adult body length, 83 to 114 centimeters.

Diet

They feed on fish eggs, jellyfish, mollusks, worms, sponges, algae, crustaceans and small invertebrates.

LEATHERBACK SEA TURTLE

Breeding

Breeding occurs between April and November. Females then lay 50 to 170 eggs. She then covers the eggs with sand after which she returns to the ocean. The young hatch after a period of 55 to 75 days and are immediately independent, receiving no parental care.

Appearance

They possess a leatherback with no visible shell. As their shell is made up of bones that are buried into its skin. The skin of leatherback sea turtle ranges in color from black to brown. Present on their backs and sides are pronounced ridges. Upon hatching, the young are usually black with their flippers having white margins. A row of white scales is present on their backs and gives the young the appearance of a white stripe running down their backs. Adults weigh 250 to 900 kilograms with females being larger than males.

Lifespan

Up to 30 years.

Length

Adult body length, 145 to 160 centimeters.

Diet

They feed on fish, marine worms, cephalopods, sea urchins, snails, jellies and zooplankton.

POND SLIDER

Breeding

Breeding occurs between April to late October but can persist until December. Females construct nests where they lay 6 to 11 eggs in a clutch. The eggs are covered and after a period of 60 to 95 days, the eggs hatch. The young are immediately independent upon hatching receiving no care from their parents. Some of the young leave the nest while others remain in the nest for up to 10 months.

Appearance

They possess oblong heads with an upward pointed snout. The upper part of their shell is oval in shape and ranges in color from brown to black to yellow to grey. It usually has yellow lines that are large in size the plastron of pond slider is lighter in color with a yellow appearance that often has black spots. They possess dark green and brown skin. In mature males, there can be darkening of the skin and the upper part of their shell. Adults weigh up to 3200 grams with females being larger than males.

Lifespan

Up to 30 years.

Length

Adult body length, females, 15 to 20 centimeters.

Adult males body length, 9 to 11 centimeters.

Diet

They feed on leaves, wood, seeds, grains, flowers, nuts, algae, eggs, fish, insects, mollusks and carrion.

OLIVE RIDLEY SEA TURTLE

Breeding

Breeding occurs from June to December. Females lay 100 to 110 eggs which she covers with sand. Once the eggs hatch, the young find their way to the water and are immediately independent receiving no parental care.

Appearance

They possess an olive-coloured outer part of their shell which is round and shaped like a heart. On the bridge of their carapace, there are scutes with each side having around 12 to 14 marginal scutes. The head of olive ridley sea turtle is medium-sized and broad while its upper parts range in color from greyish-green to olive. The young are usually dark grey and a thin white line forms a border on their carapace and trails the edge of their flippers. Their posterior scutes are serrated. Adults weigh between 25 to 46 kilograms.

Lifespan

About 50 years.

Length

Adult body length, 62 to 70 centimeters.

Diet

They feed on crabs, lobsters, mollusks, turnicates, fish, shrimp, snails, seaweed and algae.

AMPHIBIANS

WOOD FROG
Breeding

Breeding occurs between March to May. Females then lay 1000 to 3000 eggs which are attached to grasses or twigs. After a period of 9 to 30 days, the eggs hatch. Tadpoles are immediately independent upon hatching and are around 2 months, they undergo metamorphosis.

Appearance

They can be brown, rust coloured, tan, grey or green in colour and have a black colouration extends over their outer ear to the base of their front leg. Outlining their upper lips is a white line. on their sides and mid-back, there is a light yellowish-brown fold. Extending on their either side from behind the eye are to their legs are two black ridges. They possess white under parts that become orange-yellow towards the rear. On the thighs of male adult frogs, there are usually bright colours. Adults weigh about 7 grams with females being larger than males.

Lifespan

About 3 to 5 years.

Length

Adult body length, 3.5 to 7.6 centimeters.

Diet

They feed on eggs, spiders, beetles, slugs, moth larvae, slugs, snails, terrestrial worms, mollusks and algae.

WESTERN TOAD
Breeding

Breeding occurs from late April to July. Females then lay their eggs communally producing up to 12000 eggs in each clutch. These are attached to vegetation in water close to the shore. The eggs hatch within a week. Upon hatching, the tadpoles are immediately independent. They undergo metamorphosis within three months.

Appearance

Western toads are dusky grey or greenish in colour with a white or cream stripe present dorsally. Their parotids are widely separated and oval. The pupils of western toad are vertical and their venter is mottled. During the breeding season males usually have reduced dorsal blotching and their forefeet possess thickened skin that is known as nuptial pads. The young lack a dorsal stripe. Adults weigh 3 to 10 grams with females being larger than males.

Lifespan

In the wild, 8 to 12 years.

Length

Adult snout to vent length, males, 6 to 11 centimeters.

Adult females, snout to vent length, 12 centimeters.

Diet

They feed on caterpillars, termites, earwigs, beetles, ants, wood, stems, bark and algae.

ROUGH-SKINNED NEWT

Breeding

Breeding occurs in late summer. Females then lay eggs which they attach to vegetation. After 3 to 4 days, these hatch into  tadpoles. Upon hatching, the tadpoles are immediately independent receiving no parental care.

Appearance

They usually have a grainy skin that has a darker colouration  dorsally and a ventral orange to yellow-orange appearance. They also possess small eyes with yellow irises while their lower eyelids are orange. The vent of males is longer than that of females. The skin of males is spongy and smooth with a lighter colouration during the breeding season and their nuptial pads and tail crests become more pronounced. Aquatic females usually have smoother skin that is lighter s compared to terrestrial females. Adults weigh about 12 grams with males being larger than females.

Lifespan

About 18 years.

Length

Adult body length, 12 to 21 centimeters.

Diet

They feed on black worms, earth worms, small crickets, slugs, ghost shrimp, spiders and blood worms.

COLUMBIA SPOTTED FROG

Breeding

Breeding occurs from late February to early July. Females then lay 150 to 500 eggs which are usually laid communally so as to increase survival chances. They hatch after 5 to 21 days. Upon hatching, tadpoles are immediately independent receiving no care from their parents. Metamorphosis occurs before fall.

Appearance

Their dorsal colouration ranges from brown to tan or olive-green and they usually have black or brown spots that are irregularly shaped. These are also present on their sides and legs and usually have lighter centers. They possess a ventral surface that is white and their lower abdomen is bright pink. Running along their upper lips is a yellowish or white stripe.

Their snout is narrow and their eyes are upturned. They also possess short legs. Adults weigh 47 to 103 grams with females being larger than males.

Lifespan

About 3 to 13 years.

Length

Adult males, 65 millimeters.

Adult females, 100 millimeters.

Diet

They feed on mollusks, earthworms, mollusks, algae and insects.

PACIFIC CHORUS FROG

Breeding

Breeding occurs around November to Jul. females lay up to 70 eggs which are laid in clusters on vegetation. Within seven days, the eggs hatch and tadpoles are immediately independent receiving no parental care. They undergo metamorphosis at around 2 to 3 months.

Appearance

Pacific chorus frogs are usually green, brown, grey, tan, reddish or cream in colour with most being green or brown in colour. They possess a dark brown or black eye-stripe that outlines their eyes and their toe tips have round pads and small webbings. Their heads are large in size and a dark mark runs from their nostrils to the shoulders. They also possess slender legs that are long. Their underside is creamy in colour and becomes yellow towards the rear. Adults weigh about 0.35 grams.

Lifespan

About 5 to 7 years in the wild.

Length

Adult body length, 3 to 4.5 centimeters.

Diet

They feed on spiders, beetles, ants, crickets, slugs and earthworms.

NORTHERN RED-LEGGED FROG
Breeding

Breeding occurs from around January to April. Females then lay 200 to 100 eggs that are attached to submerged vegetation. These hatch within 39 to 45 days. Upon hatching, tadpoles are independent receiving no care from their parents. They undergo metamorphosis within 80 days.

Appearance

They are reddish brown to grey in colour and usually have numerous dark specks and blotches that are poorly defined. These are often absent at the top of their heads and on their backs. Present on its jaws bordering its dark mask is a light stripe. On their backs and sides, they have folds. Their undersides have a yellow colouration with the lower abdomen and hind legs having a red colouration. The forearms of males are usually enlarged. The skin of these frogs is rough in texture with their dorsal surface having light centered spots.

Lifespan

About 15 years.

Length

Adult body length, 2 to 5 inches.

Diet

They feed on beetles, snails, worms, tadpoles, fish, crustaceans, spiders and mollusks.

LONG-TOED SALAMANDER
Breeding

Breeding occurs in January. Females then lay 6 to 8 eggs which are left to hatch on their own. The eggs hatch into tadpoles within 4 to 12 weeks, at around March. Upon hatching, the tadpoles are immediately independent receiving no care from

their parents. They undergo metamorphosis and become adult salamanders.

Appearance

They are yellow in colour but some may have a red appearance. They possess large tails that usually comprise of up to 60 percent of their entire body length. Their eyes are large while their bodies are slender with stout limbs. Their belly ranges in colour from cream to light yellow. The larvae of long-tailed salamander usually possess branching gills, tail fins and a cream coloured dorsal colouration and are aquatic.

Lifespan

In the wild, 5 to 10 years.

Length

Adult body length, 100 to 200 millimeters.

Diet

They feed on spiders, beetles, butterflies, moths and terrestrial worms.

NORTHWESTERN SALAMANDER

Breeding

Breeding occurs once yearly, between January and May. Females lay eggs at around January to May and these are usually attached to vegetation. About a month later, the offspring emerges. The number of young ones ranges from 40 to 270. Upon hatching, the young receive no parental care. After one to two years, they metamorphose into their terrestrial form.

Appearance

North western salamanders are olive-green to brown in colour with dark grey to pale white ventral colouration. On their dorsum, there can be blotches and smooth brown to dark brown colouration and along their sides, they usually have  yellow flecks. Their ventral skin is light brown in colour. Behind each eye, there are parotid glands which appear as swellings. Salamanders living on land may have small, light-coloured blotches on their dorsum that are irregular.

Lifespan

About 5 years.

Length

Adult body length, 14 to 22 centimeters.

Diet

They feed on mites, amphipods, eggs, ostracods, mollusks, annelids, arthropods and dipterans.

PLANTS

FIREWEED

Description

It is a herbaceous perennial plant with spirally arranged leaves. Its stem is reddish and it produces flowers that are about 2 to 3 centimeters in diameter with its flowers ranging in colour from white to pink to magenta petals. These flowers are arranged in an elongated cluster It usually grows to a height of 0.5 to 2.5 meters.

Fruit

It produces a brown tubular seed capsule that releases a vast amount of seeds that have wispy hairs which they use to fly.

Uses

Its leaves were used to make tea and its shoots were used as vegetable. The flowers of fireweed produce nectar that is used to make spicy honey and its honey, syrup and jelly are popular in Alaska.

DEVIL'S CLUB

Description

Devil's club is a deciduous shrub whose stem has a lot of spines and is sparsely branched. The leaves of Devil's club are large and broad with a shape that resembles that of maple leaves. They possess numerous spines underneath. Devil's club produces white flowers that are small in size. It grows to a height of 1 to 3 meters.

Fruit

They produce small berries that are bright red and these grow in clusters that are pyramid-shaped. These berries are not edible to human beings.

Uses

The charcoal from its stalks is used to make protective and ceremonial face paints. The plant was used as traditional medicine for rheumatoid arthritis and adult onset diabetes mellitus. It was also used as oral tea and as ointments and poultices. Its dried and powdered bark was used as a deodorant and was added in mashed berries and used in cleaning hair. Extracts of this plant have been found to have the potential to inhibit tuberculosis. Its berries are eaten by animals.

COMMON YARROW
Description

It is a perennial plant that is hardy with aromatic fine leaves that have a feathery cut with a fern-like appearance measuring 4 to 15 centimetres long. It bears clusters of small white flowers that can be pink. These appear around April to October. It grows to a height of around 1 meter.

Fruit

The fruit of common yarrow is small in size, flattened, dry and hard.

Uses

It was used as medicine traditionally. Its crushed leaves were used to stop bleeding and heal wounds as well as in stopping nose bleed. It was chewed as treatment for toothaches and its infusion was used to treat earaches. It was also used as an eye wash, analgesic and in treating headaches. The plant is edible especially its young leaves. It can also be used in drying wool.

RED-BERRIED ELDER
Description

It is a shrub that produces large branching clusters of flowers that range in colour from cream to white. These are usually saucer shaped. When flower buds are closed, the flowers have a pink colouration which ranges from yellowish, cream to white when open. It is deciduous with compound leaves that are pinnate. They grow to a height of 2 to 6 meters.

Fruit

It produces red berries that usually have 3 to 5 stone-like seeds. These appear starting from mid-July to August.

Uses

Its fruit is edible when cooked and was used to make wine. In cases of poisoning, the plant was traditionally used as an emetic. Its roots were rubbed on the skin whenever one had muscle ache. Birds feed on its berries and insects obtain nectar from its flowers.

WESTERN BUNCHBERRY

Description

This plant bears 4 to 6 leaves that have smooth-edges at the stem summit. These usually have whitish appearance beneath and a green appearance on top. They have an oblong shape and produce four bracts that are creamy-white which surround a button-like disc. Their stems grow to a height of 8 to 15 meters it expands via rhizomes and grows tucked beneath shrubs.

Fruit

They produce brilliant scarlet red fruits in August. They usually contain 1 to 2 seeds.

Uses

Its roots have been used as a cold remedy and its berries were preserved and eaten in winter. Its bark was used as a laxative it can also be used as an analgesic and an anti-inflammatory agent. Its berries have been used in making plum pudding.

LARKSPURLEAF MONKSHOOD

Description

It is a perennial plant with a narrow stem whose leaves alternate. Its leaves have five lobes that are deeply divided with each having three small lobes. The flowers of larkspur leaf monkshood range in colour from dark blue to purple and around 3 to 15 flowers are usually present on the stem. The blossoms of these flowers are usually green-yellow at first. This plant grows to a height of 0.3 to 1 meter.

Fruit

Its fruit is an aggregate of follicles that are made up of dry structures with numerous seeds.

Uses

In traditional medicine, it was used in treatment of fever and pain. The plant was also used as poison historically and can be poisonous to both humans and animals. It has also been used in floral arrangements by florists.

LINGONBERRY
Description

This plant has cross-sectionally rounded stems with leaves growing in an alternating pattern. Its leaves are oval and have a slightly wavy margin. The flowers of lingonberry are shaped like a bell and their colour ranges from pale pink to white. These flowers are about 3 to 8 millimeters in length and are mostly produced in summer. These plants grow to a height of about 10 to 40 centimeters.

Fruit

The fruit of lingon berry is a berry that is red in colour.

Uses

In traditional medicine, the berries were used as treatment for minor respiratory conditions. The berries are edible and are often cooked and sweetened prior to consumption in form of jam, juice or syrup. A traditional soft drink made from it known as lingonberry water was used as a laxative. Firm ripe berries were added to strings and worn as necklaces and they were also used to colour the quills of porcupines.

NOOTKA LUPINE
Description

It is a perennial herbaceous plant with stout hairy stems. It produces palmate compound leaves with 6 to 9 leaves. Its flowers are pea-like and range in colour from blue to violet. The flowers grow in dense clusters on top of the stem. The flowers grow to 2 centimeters long. It grows to 0.5 to 1.2 meters tall.

Fruit

Its fruit is a brown pea-like pod that is about 2 centimeters long.

Uses

Bears consume the roots of nootka lupine. Its roots were roasted and cooked and its seeds were used as a protein rich vegetable. The seeds of nootka lupine were roasted or ground to form a powder.

STAIRSTEP MOSS
Description

These plants usually have an olive green colouration and their stems and branches are red in colour. They form branches that are up to 20 centimeters long. It produces fern-like shoots that usually have numerous branches with stems that have a reddish appearance. This plant loves growing in shaded areas and produces feathery fronds in steps each year.

Uses

It is used for commercial purposes in floral exhibitions. It is useful in lining fruit storage boxes. It was used to cover dirt floors. It is used in log cabins to fill spaces between logs. The plant also has antibacterial properties.

SITKA SPRUCE
Description

It is a large tree with light green to bluish green needle-like leaves which are usually arranged spirally on the twig. The bark of Sitka spruce is thin and has a scaly appearance with its inner bark having a reddish-brown colouration. Mature trees usually have a cylindrical crown while younger trees have a conical crown. Older trees usually have their branches starting from high up the tree. It grows to a height of 90 meters and measures about 2 meters in diameter.

Fruit

They produce cones that are pale green initially and ripen to become pale creamy brown.

Uses

The wood of Sitka spruce is used in making paper especially wood from young trees. Wood from mature trees is used in making ships, airplane framework components, pianos, guitars, violins and boats. Its inner bark can be used as a laxative and its pitch can be used as a salve to skin ailments, boils and burns. Its roots are used to make baskets, ropes and fishing lines.

WESTERN HEMLOCK
Description

It is a large evergreen tree with a brown bark that is thin and furrowed. Its crown usually has a cylindrical shape in mature trees and a conical shape in young trees. As the tree matures, it self-prunes and its branches start from high up. Its leaves are needle-like, long and flattened in cross-section. On their upper surface, they range from mid to dark green. Leaves are usually arranged spirally and are twisted at the base such that they lie on either side of the shoot. These trees grow to a height of 50 to 70 meters and a diameter of around 2.7 meters.

Fruit

They produce green cones that become brown upon maturity.

Uses

It is used as an ornamental tree in gardens. On river banks, it helps to prevent soil erosion. It is used to make timber and paper and in making furniture and doors. Its fiber is used to make plastic and rayon. Its inner bark was consumed as emergency food and its bark was cooked so as to make medicinal extracts that were used in the treatment of tuberculosis, haemorrhage and fever. Its new growth needles can be chewed directly or be made to bitter tea.

NOOTKA CYPRESS

Description

Nootka cypress is an evergreen tree that usually has a thin smooth bark which is flaky and grey on mature trees and purplish on young trees. It possesses dark green scale-like leaves that are about 3 to 5 millimeters long. It grows up to a height of 40 to 60 meters and ranges in diameter from 3 to 4 meters.

Fruit

It produces cones that are small in size and hard. These are initially green but ripen in the second year.

Uses

Its wood is used during shipbuilding and building boats and furniture.it was used for sweet baths in treatment of rheumatism and arthritis and its infusion was used to wash swellings and sores. Its soft bark was used to cover poultices.

TREMBLING ASPEN
Description

It is a tall tree with a smooth bark that is light green in young trees and becomes whitish as the tree matures. These trees usually have thick black scars horizontally and prominent knots that are black. The leaves of these trees are almost round in shape and are green above and grey below. Younger trees usually have larger triangular shaped leaves. There are separate male and female cones and these plants produce catkins as flowers. These catkins are around 4 to 6 centimeters long and precede the production of leaves. These trees grow to a height of 15 to 18 meters and about 25 centimeters diameter.

Fruit

Their fruit is usually a long pendulous string of capsules that measures up to 10 centimeters in length. Each of their capsules usually has cotton fluff around them to assist in their dispersal.

Uses

Its bark contains a substance that was used as a substitute for quinine. It is also used as a source of poor fuel wood. Its wood is used for pulp products and in making furniture boxes, wall panels, crates and boxes.

BOG MYRTLE
Description

It is a deciduous shrub with spirally arranged leaves that are about 2 to 5 centimeters long with a broad tip and a tapered base. Its leaf margins are finely toothed. It produces catkins as flowers and male and female flowers are usually on different plants. These plants grow to a height of 1 to 2 meters.

Fruit

Its fruit is a small drupe that is indehiscent. This fruit is around 3 millimeters in diameter and bears a single large seed.

Uses

Its foliage was used traditionally as an insect repellent. It was also used as a condiment and in perfumery in royal wedding bouquets. Its leaves can be dried and can be used in making tea and seasoning. It was used as flavouring for beer in the past and as a traditional form of treatment for stomach aches, fever, liver problems and bronchial ailments.

ALASKA PAPER BIRCH
Description

The leaves of Alaska paper birch range in shape from triangular to oval with long-tapered tips and a broad wedge shaped base. Their lower surface is usually yellowish-green while its upper surface is shiny dark green. The margins of these leaves are smooth with the leaves measuring about 4 to 7 centimeters in length. The barks of Alaska paper birch are a bright reddish-brown when young and mature to become creamy white or pink. Alaska paper birch produces catkins as flowers. Their pollen catkins are about 2 to 4 centimeters long while seed catkins are 1 to 2 centimeters long. It grows to a height of 15 meters and measures up to 20 centimeters in diameter.

Fruit

Their fruit is usually scales with 2 lateral lobes that are rounded and point away from the central lobe

Uses

It is used as a source of firewood and in making furniture, plywood, spears, bows, arrows and sleds. It is useful in making pulpwood for manufacturing paper. Its sap is usually boiled to produce syrup and its bark is a good fire starter. It was used in making canoes, containers and wigwams.

WESTERN RED CEDAR
Description

it is a tall evergreen tree with small, scale-like leaves that have an ovate shape. These are usually 2 to 3 millimeters long and have a dark glossy green appearance above while underneath, they have whitish markings. Both male and female flowers usually grow on the same plant with male cones being small and hardly noticeable. Female cones being small, reddish purple and are usually located near tips of branches. These trees grow to a height of 65 meters.

Fruit

Its fruit is small cones that are woody and brown in colour. These are usually oval in shape and slender with scales. They possess narrow wings on both sides.

Uses

The wood of western cedar is used in roofing and in making of fence posts, utility poles, paper pulp and various containers. Its leaves are used as food by animals. Its bark was used to make skirts, dresses and caps and its roots and limbs were used in making ropes and basket. The tree also has medicinal value.

BEBB'S WILLOW

Description

It is a large shrub with elliptical leaves that are one to three inches long. When young, its leaves are hairy and when they mature, they become strong veined. The bark of bebb's willow is red in colour, thin and olive-green and at times it is grey with a tinge of red and is divided by shallow fissures. Its roots are usually shallow. It grows to a height of up to 10 feet.

Fruit

Its fruit is usually capsules that are 6 to 8 millimeters long with long beaks and sparse hairs.

Uses

A poultice made from its inner bark was applied to the skin over a broken bone and a poultice made from its bark and sap was applied as wad on to bleeding wounds. Its diamond-shaped wood is used in carving lampposts, furniture, baskets, baseball bats, canes and in making charcoal and gunpowder. Wild animals usually browse its leaves and birds feed on its buds.

TEALEAF WILLOW
Description

Tealeaf willow is an upright plant with multiple stems and it is deciduous. Flowering occurs between May and June. It grows to a height of 3 to 6 feet. It is found growing above the timberline in interior Alaska and in northern Alaska, it grows at the timberline. Male and female flowers grow on separate plants. The flowers are usually catkin scales that have a rounded tip and they are stalk less and short.

Fruit

The fruit of tealeaf willow is a two valved silky capsule that is around 8 millimeters long.

Uses

Its leaves and shoots were eaten raw or dried or stored for future use in seal oil. Its leaves were useful in brewing tea and in making soup. Parts of the plant were chewed as treatment for mouth sores and pain. Some of its parts were used in basket weaving and in making arrows and bows. Its parts were also used in the making of animal traps.

PALE PAINTBRUSH
Description

It is a perennial herbaceous plant and usually bears a number of stems which either grow straight upwards or curve from the base outwards. Its stem is covered in glandular hairs .It produces leaves that range in colour from green to purple and are spear-head shaped and broad. This plant flowers from May to September and its pale yellow-green inflorescences are 2 to 11 centimeters tall and 1 to 4 centimeters wide. At the point where the bracts attach to the stem, they are sulphurous yellow to green with cream, white or yellow canary tips. Near the base, they can have a brown to purple colouration. Pale paintbrush grows to 22 to 55 centimeters high.

Fruit

It produces fruit capsules that are embedded with a large number of seeds.

Uses

Its bracts were used for medicinal purposes and its top half collected as food. The plant was crushed and put in open wounds or skin conditions so as to promote healing. The combination of nutrients present in the plant can be used to shrink tumours.